The
Treasury
of
Best-Loved
Poems

The
Treasury
of
Best-Loved
Poems

SECOND EDITION

EDITED BY
Louis Phillips

ISBN 0-679-77703-2

Designed by Beth Tondreau Design/Mary A. Wirth

Printed and Typeset in the United States of America
0 9 8 7 6 5 4 3
Special Edition

Contents

Introduction

There is an old rhyme that goes:

Come on in,
The water's fine.
I'll give you
Till I count to nine.
If you're not
In by then,
Guess I'll have to
Count to ten.

This is my invitation to all readers—"Come on in. The water's fine." Amid these pages you will encounter verses wise, verses funny, verses witty, verses sentimental, verses strange, and verses sad. You will encounter poems to move you, to amuse you—poems to add zest to the mysterious process of living.

How truly wonderful it is to hold one special verse close to your heart—to memorize the lines and recite them to yourself or to others for comfort or for pleasure. I remember quite vividly watching my own father standing up in the living room to recite Robert Service's classic ballad "The Shooting of Dan McGrew." My father would grow quite serious and then with dramatic flair the lines would flow and soar as my sisters and I listened with amazement. Why would a man who rarely read serious novels or poetry memorize so many lines? Why would he want to? I never knew the answer, but I do know that few performances entertained me quite so much.

Thus, the poems in this anthology have been collected for a wide variety of reasons. Some verses have been truly popular. Some have historical significance. Some catch a fleeting moment of American life. Some, such as "The Shooting of Dan McGrew," have personal significance for me. Some are new and should be loved. There are as many reasons for loving a particular poem as there are poems to love.

In this computer age we might find it strange to think of poems being loved at all. In an age dominated by television, motion pictures, and spreadsheets, what relevance does poetry have to our lives?

All you have to do is read some poetry to know the answer. True poets speak to us about what we feel and think and use the talents God has given them to create and re-create manifold experiences. Poetry exists in a language akin to music, in lines related to the mysterious, and somehow, in spite of everything, reminds us how important it is to speak honestly and memorably about our lives.

And so come on in. The water's fine.

— Louis Phillips

· O N E ·

The World
of
Love and
Romance

The Passionate Shepherd to His Love

Come live with me, and be my love;
And we will all the pleasures prove
That hills and valleys, dales and fields,
Woods, or steepy mountain yields.

And we will sit upon the rocks,
Seeing the shepherds feed their flocks
By shallow rivers, to whose falls
Melodious birds sing madrigals.

And I will make thee beds of roses,
And a thousand fragrant posies;
A cap of flowers, and a kirtle
Embroidered all with leaves of myrtle;

A gown made of the finest wool
Which from our pretty lambs we pull;
Fair-lined slippers for the cold,
With buckles of the purest gold;

A belt of straw and ivy-buds,
With coral clasps and amber studs;
And if these pleasures may thee move,
Come live with me, and be my love.

The shepherd-swains shall dance and sing
For thy delight each May morning;
If these delights thy mind may move,
Then live with me, and be my love.

— CHRISTOPHER MARLOWE

On Bundling

Since in bed, a maid
May bundle and be chaste.
It doth no good to burn up wood.
It is a needless waste.

— ANONYMOUS

To the Virgins, to Make Much of Time

Gather ye rosebuds while ye may,
    Old Time is still a-flying;
And this same flower that smiles to-day
    To-morrow will be dying.

The glorious lamp of heaven, the Sun,
  The higher he's a-getting,
The sooner will his race be run,
  And nearer he's to setting.

That age is best which is the first,
  When youth and blood are warmer;
But being spent, the worse, and worst
  Times still succeed the former.

Then be not coy, but use your time;
  And while ye may, go marry;
For having lost but once your prime,
  You may forever tarry.

— ROBERT HERRICK

Careless Love

Love, O love, O careless love,
You see what careless love can do.
When I wore my apron low,
Couldn't keep you from my door,
  Fare you well, fare you well.

Now I wear my apron high.
Scarce see you passin' by,
   Fare you well, fare you well.

— ANONYMOUS

Western Wind

Western wind, when wilt thou blow,
The small rain down can rain?
Christ, if my love were in my arms,
And I in my bed again!

— ANONYMOUS

Believe Me, If All Those Endearing Young Charms

Believe me, if all those endearing young
   charms,
Which I gaze on so fondly today,

Were to change by tomorrow, and fleet in my
    arms,
  Like fairy-gifts fading away,
Thou wouldst still be adored, as this moment
    thou art,
  Let thy loveliness fade as it will,
And around the dear ruin each wish of my
    heart
Would entwine itself verdantly still.

It is not while beauty and youth are thine
    own,
  And thy cheeks unprofaned by a tear
That the fervor and faith of a soul can be
    known,
  To which time will but make thee more
    dear;
No, the heart that has truly loved never
    forgets,
  But as truly loves on to the close,
As the sunflower turns on her god, when he
    sets,
  The same look which she turned when he
    rose.

— THOMAS MOORE

To His Coy Mistress

Had we but world enough, and time,
This coyness, Lady, were no crime.
We would sit down and think which way
To walk and pass our long love's day,
Thou by the Indian Ganges' side
Shouldst rubies find; I by the tide
Of Humber would complain. I would
Love you ten years before the Flood,
And you should, if you please, refuse
Till the conversion of the Jews.
My vegetable love should grow
Vaster than empires, and more slow;
An hundred years should go to praise
Thine eyes and on thy forehead gaze;
Two hundred to adore each breast,
But thirty thousand to the rest;
An age at least to every part,
And the last age should show your heart.
For, Lady, you deserve this state,
Nor would I love at lower rate.
   But at my back I always hear
Time's wingèd chariot hurrying near;
And yonder all before us lie
Deserts of vast eternity.
Thy beauty shall no more be found,

Nor, in thy marble vault, shall sound
My echoing song; then worms shall try
That long preserved virginity,
And your quaint honor turn to dust,
And into ashes all my lust:
The grave's a fine and private place,
But none, I think, do there embrace.
  Now therefore, while the youthful hue
Sits on thy skin like morning dew,
And while thy willing soul transpires
At every pore with instant fires,
Now let us sport us while we may,
And now, like amorous birds of prey,
Rather at once our time devour
Than languish in his slow-chapped power.
Let us roll all our strength and all
Our sweetness up into one ball,
And tear our pleasures with rough strife
Through the iron gates of life:
Thus, though we cannot make our sun
Stand still, yet we will make him run.

— ANDREW MARVELL

Shall I Compare Thee

Shall I compare thee to a summer's day?
Thou art more lovely and more temperate:
Rough winds do shake the darling buds of
    May,
And summer's lease hath all too short a date·
Sometime too hot the eye of heaven shines,
And often is his gold complexion dimmed;
And every fair from fair sometimes declines,
By chance, or nature's changing course
    untrimmed;
But thy eternal summer shall not fade,
Nor lose possession of that fair thou owest;
Nor shall Death brag thou wanderest in his
    shade
When in eternal lines to time thou growest:
So long as men can breathe, or eyes can see,
So long lives this, and this gives life to thee.

— WILLIAM SHAKESPEARE

My Mistress' Eyes

My mistress' eyes are nothing like the sun;
Coral is far more red than her lips' red:
If snow be white, why then her breasts are
     dun;
If hairs be wires, black wires grow on her
     head.
I have seen roses damasked, red and white,
But no such roses see I in her cheeks;
And in some perfumes is there more delight
Than in the breath that from my mistress
     reeks.
I love to hear her speak, yet well I know
That music hath a far more pleasing sound:
I grant I never saw a goddess go,—
My mistress, when she walks, treads on the
     ground.
And yet, by heaven, I think my love as rare
As any she belied with false compare.

— WILLIAM SHAKESPEARE

Oh, Dear! What Can the Matter Be?

Oh, dear! What can the matter be? Jonny's so
      long at the fair!
He promised to buy me a trinket to please me!
And then for a smile, Oh he vowed he would
      tease me.
He promised to bring me a bunch of blue
      ribbons to tie up my bonnie brown hair.

Perhaps he thought our meeting was another
      day!
Perhaps he wandered all around and lost his
      way!
Or perhaps he's looking up and down
And here and there and everywhere
To find the finest ribbons for my bonnie hair.

He promised to bring me a basket of posies,
A garland of lilies, a gift of red roses,
A little straw hat to set off the blue ribbons
      that tie up my bonnie brown hair!
Oh, dear! What can the matter be?
      Jonny's so long at the fair!

— ANONYMOUS

He's Gone Away

He's gone away for to stay a little while
But he's comin' back if he goes ten thousand
      miles.
Oh who will tie my shoes? Oh who will glove
      my hand?
And who will kiss my ruby lips when he is
      gone?
Look away over yondro.

He's gone away for to stay a little while
But he's comin' back if he goes ten thousand
      miles.
Oh it's pappy'll tie my shoes
      and mammy'll glove my hands.
And you will kiss my ruby lips when you
      come back!
Look away over yondro.

— TRADITIONAL FOLK SONG

My Luve's Like a Red, Red Rose

O my Luve's like a red, red rose,
　That's newly sprung in June:
O my Luve's like the melodie
　That's sweetly played in tune!

As fair art thou, my bonnie lass,
　So deep in luve am I;
And I will luve thee still, my dear,
　Till a' the seas gang dry.

Till a' the seas gang dry, my dear,
　And the rocks melt wi' the sun;
I will luve thee still, my dear,
　While the sands o' life shall run.

And fare thee weel, my only Luve,
　And fare thee weel a while!
And I will come again, my Luve,
　Though it were ten thousand mile.

— ROBERT BURNS

She Walks in Beauty

She walks in beauty, like the night
  Of cloudless climes and starry skies;
And all that's best of dark and bright
  Meet in her aspect and her eyes:
Thus mellowed to that tender light
  Which heaven to gaudy day denies.

One shade the more, one ray the less,
  Had half impaired the nameless grace
Which waves in every raven tress,
  Or softly lightens o'er her face;
Where thoughts serenely sweet express
  How pure, how dear their dwelling place.

And on that cheek, and o'er that brow,
  So soft, so calm, yet eloquent,
The smiles that win, the tints that glow,
  But tell of days in goodness spent,
A mind at peace with all below,
  A heart whose love is innocent!

— GEORGE GORDON, LORD BYRON

Outwitted

He drew a circle that shut me out—
Heretic, rebel, a thing to flout.
But Love and I had the wit to win:
We drew a circle that took him in!

— EDWIN MARKHAM

Billy Boy

Oh, where have you been, Billy boy, Billy
    boy,
Oh, where have you been, charming Billy?
I have been to seek a wife, she's the joy of my
    young life,
She's a young thing and cannot leave her
    mother.

Did she ask you to come in, Billy boy, Billy
  boy,
Did she ask you to come in, charming Billy?
She did ask me to come in, with a dimple in
  her chin,
She's a young thing and cannot leave her
  mother.

Did she ask you to sit down, Billy boy, Billy
  boy,
Did she ask you to sit down, charming Billy?
She did ask me to sit down, with a curtsey to
  the ground,
She's a young thing and cannot leave her
  mother.

Did she set for you a chair, Billy boy, Billy
  boy,
Did she set for you a chair, charming Billy?
Yes, she set for me a chair, she's got ringlets
  in her hair,
She's a young thing and cannot leave her
  mother.

How old is she, Billy boy, Billy boy,
How old is she, charming Billy?

She's three times six, four times seven,
    twenty-eight, and eleven,
She's a young thing and cannot leave her
    mother.
How tall is she, Billy boy, Billy boy,
How tall is she, charming Billy?
She's as tall as any pine and as straight's a
    pumpkin vine,
She's a young thing and cannot leave her
    mother.

Can she make a cherry pie, Billy boy, Billy
    boy,
Can she make a cherry pie, charming Billy?
She can make a cherry pie, quick's a cat can
    wink her eye,
She's a young thing and cannot leave her
    mother.

Does she often go to church, Billy boy, Billy
    boy,
Does she often go to church, charming Billy?
Yes, she often goes to church, with her
    bonnet white as birch,
She's a young thing and cannot leave her
    mother.

Can she make a pudding well, Billy boy,
　　Billy boy,
Can she make a pudding well, charming
　　Billy?
She can make a pudding well, I can tell it by
　　the smell,
She's a young thing and cannot leave her
　　mother.

Can she make a feather-bed, Billy boy, Billy
　　boy,
Can she make a feather-bed, charming Billy?
She can make a feather-bed, place the pillows
　　at the head,
She's a young thing and cannot leave her
　　mother.

Can she card and can she spin, Billy boy,
　　Billy boy,
Can she card and can she spin, charming
　　Billy?
She can card and she can spin, she can do
　　most anything,
She's a young thing and cannot leave her
　　mother.

— Anonymous

19

How Do I Love Thee?

How do I love thee? Let me count the ways.
I love thee to the depth and breadth and
      height
My soul can reach, when feeling out of sight
For the Ends of Being and ideal Grace.
I love thee to the level of everyday's
Most quiet need, by sun and candle-light.
I love thee freely, as men strive for Right;
I love thee purely, as they turn from Praise.
I love thee with the passion put to use
In my old griefs, and with my childhood's
      faith.
I love thee with a love I seemed to lose
With my lost saints,—I love thee with the
      breath,
Smiles, tears, of all my life!—and, if God
      choose,
I shall but love thee better after death.

— ELIZABETH BARRETT BROWNING

Cuna Love Song

Many pretty flowers, red, blue,
   and yellow; we say to the girls,
"Let's go and walk among the
   flowers."
The wind comes and sways the
   flowers, the girls are like that
   when they dance; some are
   wide open, large flowers and
   some are tiny little flowers.
The birds love the sunshine and
   the starlight; the flowers smell
   sweet.
The girls are sweeter than the
   flowers.

— ANONYMOUS (Native American)

21

What Lips My Lips Have Kissed, and Where, and Why

What lips my lips have kissed, and where,
    and why,
I have forgotten, and what arms have lain
Under my head till morning; but the rain
Is full of ghosts tonight, that tap and sigh
Upon the glass and listen for reply,
And in my heart there stirs a quiet pain
For unremembered lads that not again
Will turn to me at midnight with a cry.
Thus in the winter stands the lonely tree,
Nor knows what birds have vanished one by
    one,
Yet knows its boughs more silent than before:
I cannot say what loves have come and gone,
I only know that summer sang in me
A little while, that in me sings no more.

— EDNA ST. VINCENT MILLAY

Down in the Valley

Down in the valley,
Valley so low,
Hang yore head over,
Hear the wind blow.
Hear the wind blow, love,
Hear the wind blow,
Hang yore head over,
Hear the wind blow.

If you don't love me,
Love whom you please,
But throw yore arms round me,
Give my heart ease.
Give my heart ease, dear,
Give my heart ease,
Throw yore arms round me,
Give my heart ease.

Down in the valley
Walking between,
Telling our story,
Here's what it sings—
Roses love sunshine,
Violets love dew,
Angels in heaven,
Know I love you.

Build me a castle,
Forty feet high,
So I can see her
As she goes by
As she goes by, dear,
As she goes by,
So I can see her,
As she goes by.

Bird in a cage, love,
Bird in a cage,
Dying for freedom,
Ever a slave,
Ever a slave, dear,
Ever a slave,
Dying for freedom,
Ever a slave.

Write me a letter;
Send it by mail;
And back it in care of
The Barbourville jail.
Barbourville jail, love,
Barbourville jail,
And back it in care of
The Barbourville jail.

— ANONYMOUS

The Sands of Dee

"Oh Mary, go and call the cattle home,
  And call the cattle home,
  And call the cattle home
 Across the sands of Dee";
The western wind was wild and dank with
    foam,
 And all alone went she.

The western tide crept up along the sand,
  And o'er and o'er the sand,
  And round and round the sand,
 As far as eye could see.
The rolling mist came down and hid the land:
 And never home came she.

"Oh! is it weed, or fish, or floating hair—
  A tress of golden hair,
  A drownèd maiden's hair
 Above the nets at sea?
Was never salmon yet that shone so fair
 Among the stakes on Dee."

They rowed her in across the rolling foam,
  The cruel crawling foam,
  The cruel hungry foam,

To her grave beside the sea:
But still the boatmen hear her call the cattle
      home
Across the sands of Dee.

— CHARLES KINGSLEY

Love's Philosophy

The fountains mingle with the river
    And the rivers with the Ocean;
The winds of Heaven mix for ever
    With a sweet emotion;
Nothing in the world is single;
    All things by a law divine
In one spirit meet and mingle.
    Why not I with thine?

See the mountains kiss high Heaven
    And the waves clasp one another;
No sister-flower would be forgiven
    If it disdained its brother;

And the sunlight clasps the earth
    And the moonbeams kiss the sea—
What is all this sweet work worth
    If thou kiss not me?

— PERCY BYSSHE SHELLEY

Patterns

I walk down the garden paths,
And all the daffodils
Are blowing, and the bright blue squills.
I walk down the patterned garden paths
In my stiff, brocaded gown.
With my powdered hair and jewelled fan,
I too am a rare
Pattern. As I wander down
The garden paths.

My dress is richly figured,
And the train
Makes a pink and silver stain
On the gravel, and the thrift
Of the borders.
Just a plate of current fashion,

Tripping by in high-heeled, ribboned shoes.
Not a softness anywhere about me,
Only whalebone and brocade.
And I sink on a seat in the shade
Of a lime tree. For my passion
Wars against the stiff brocade.
The daffodils and squills
Flutter in the breeze
As they please.
And I weep;
For the lime tree is in blossom
And one small flower has dropped upon my
          bosom.

And the plashing of waterdrops
In the marble fountain
Comes down the garden paths.
The dripping never stops.
Underneath my stiffened gown
Is the softness of a woman bathing in a
          marble basin,
A basin in the midst of hedges grown
So thick, she cannot see her lover hiding,
But she guesses he is near,
And the sliding of the water
Seems the stroking of a dear
Hand upon her.

What is Summer in a fine brocaded gown!
I should like to see it lying in a heap upon
     the ground.
All the pink and silver crumpled up on the
     ground.
I would be the pink and silver as I ran along
     the paths,
And he would stumble after,
Bewildered by my laughter.
I should see the sun flashing from his sword-
     hilt and the buckles on his shoes.
I would choose
To lead him in a maze along the patterned
     paths,
A bright and laughing maze for my heavy-
     booted lover,
Till he caught me in the shade,
And the buttons of his waistcoat bruised my
     body as he clasped me,
Aching, melting, unafraid.
With the shadows of the leaves and the
     sundrops,
And the plopping of the waterdrops,
All about us in the open afternoon—
I am very like to swoon
With the weight of this brocade,
For the sun sifts through the shade.

. . .

Underneath the fallen blossom
In my bosom,
Is a letter I have hid.
It was brought to me this morning by a rider
    from the Duke.
"Madam, we regret to inform you that Lord
    Hartwell
Died in action Thursday se'nnight."
As I read it in the white, morning sunlight,
The letters squirmed like snakes.
"Any answer, Madam" said my footman.
"No," I told him.
"See that the messenger takes some
    refreshment.
No, no answer."
And I walked into the garden,
Up and down the patterned paths,
In my stiff, correct brocade.
The blue and yellow flowers stood up
    proudly in the sun,
Each one.
I stood upright too,
Held rigid to the pattern
By the stiffness of my gown.
Up and down I walked,
Up and down.

. . .

In a month he would have been my husband.
In a month, here, underneath this lime,
We would have broke the pattern;
He for me, and I for him,
He as Colonel, I as Lady,
On this shady seat.
He had a whim
That sunlight carried blessing.
And I answered, "It shall be as you have
     said."
Now he is dead.

In Summer and in Winter I shall walk
Up and down
The patterned garden paths
In my stiff, brocaded gown.
The squills and daffodils
Will give place to pillared roses, and to asters,
     and to snow.
I shall go
Up and down,
In my gown.
Gorgeously arrayed,
Boned and stayed.
And the softness of my body will be guarded
     from embrace

By each button, hook, and lace.
For the man who should loose me is dead,
Fighting with the Duke of Flanders
In a pattern called a war.
Christ! What are patterns for?

— AMY LOWELL

Oh, Rare Harry Parry

Oh, rare Harry Parry,
When will you marry?
When apples and pears are ripe.
  I'll come to your wedding
  Without any bidding,
And dance and sing all the night.

— ANONYMOUS

Jeanie with the Light Brown Hair

I dream of Jeanie with the light brown hair,
Borne like a vapor on summer air;
I see her tripping where the bright streams
        play,
Happy as the daisies that dance on her way.
Many were the wild notes her merry voice
        would pour,
Many were the blithe birds that warbled them
        o'er.
Oh! I dream of Jeanie with the light brown
        hair,
Floating like a vapor on the soft summer air.

I long for Jeanie with the day dawn smile,
Radiant in gladness, warm with winning
        guile;
I hear her melodies, like joys gone by,
Sighing 'round my heart o'er the fond hopes
        that die:
Sighing like the night wind and sobbing like
        the rain,
Wailing for the lost one that comes not again:
Oh! I long for Jeanie and my heart bows low,
Never more to find her where the bright
        waters flow.

I sigh for Jeanie, but her light form strayed
Far from the fond hearts 'round her native
    glade;
Her smiles have vanished and her sweet
    songs flown,
Flitting like the dreams that have cheered us
    and gone.
Now the nodding wild flow'rs may wither on
    the shore
While her gentle fingers will cull them no
    more:
Oh! I sigh for Jeanie with the light brown
    hair,
Floating, like a vapor, on the soft summer air.

— STEPHEN FOSTER

❧

Wait Till the Sun Shines, Nellie

On a Sunday morning sat a maid forlorn,
With her sweetheart by her side;
Thro' the window pane,
She looked at the rain,
"We must stay home, Joe," she cried;
"There's a picnic too,
At the Old Point View,
It's a shame it rained today."
Then the boy drew near,
Kissed away each tear,
And heard him softly say:
"Wait till the sun shines, Nellie,
When the clouds go drifting by.
We will be happy, Nellie,
Don't you sigh;
Down lovers' lane we'll wander,
Sweetheart, you and I;
Wait till the sun shines, Nellie,
Bye and bye."

— ANDREW B. STERLING

Nature,
the Seasons,
and the
Passing of
Time

Nature

As a fond mother, when the day is o'er,
Leads by the hand her little child to bed,
Half willing, half reluctant to be led,
And leave his broken playthings on the floor,
Still gazing at them through the open door,
Nor wholly reassured and comforted
By promises of others in their stead,
Which, though more splendid, may not please
     him more;
So Nature deals with us, and takes away
Our playthings one by one, and by the hand
Leads us to rest so gently, that we go
Scarce knowing if we wish to go or stay,
Being too full of sleep to understand
How far the unknown transcends the what we
     know.

— HENRY WADSWORTH
LONGFELLOW

I Wandered Lonely as a Cloud

I wandered lonely as a cloud
That floats on high o'er vales and hills,
When all at once I saw a crowd,
A host, of golden daffodils;
Beside the lake, beneath the trees,
Fluttering and dancing in the breeze.

Continuous as the stars that shine
And twinkle on the Milky Way,
They stretched in never-ending line
Along the margin of a bay:
Ten thousand saw I at a glance,
Tossing their heads in sprightly dance.

The waves beside them danced; but they
Outdid the sparkling waves in glee;
A poet could not but be gay,
In such a jocund company;
I gazed—and gazed—but little thought
What wealth the show to me had brought:

For oft, when on my couch I lie
In vacant or in pensive mood,
They flash upon that inward eye

Which is the bliss of solitude;
And then my heart with pleasure fills,
And dances with the daffodils.

— WILLIAM WORDSWORTH

The Year's at the Spring

The year's at the spring
And the day's at the morn;
Morning's at seven;
The hillside's dew-pearled;
The lark's on the wing;
The snail's on the thorn:
God's in his heaven—
All's right with the world!

— ROBERT BROWNING

Spring

When daffodils begin to peer,
   With heigh! the doxy, over the dale,
Why, then comes in the sweet o' the year;
   For the red blood reigns in the winter's
      pale.

The white sheet bleaching on the hedge,
   With heigh! the sweet birds, O, how they
      sing!
Doth set my pugging tooth on edge,
   For a quart of ale is a dish for a king.

The lark, that tirra-lirra chants,
   With heigh! with heigh! the thrush and the
      jay,
Are summer songs for me and my aunts,
   While we lie tumbling in the hay.

— WILLIAM SHAKESPEARE

Loveliest of Trees

Loveliest of trees, the cherry now
Is hung with bloom along the bough,
And stands about the woodland ride
Wearing white for Eastertide.

Now, of my threescore years and ten,
Twenty will not come again,
And take from seventy springs a score,
It only leaves me fifty more.

And since to look at things in bloom
Fifty springs are little room,
About the woodlands I will go
To see the cherry hung with snow.

— A. E. HOUSMAN

Serenade

Stars of the summer night!
Far in yon azure deeps,
Hide, hide your golden light!

43

She sleeps!
My lady sleeps!
Sleeps!

Moon of the summer night!
Far down yon western steeps,
Sink, sink in silver light!
She sleeps!
My lady sleeps!
Sleeps!

Wind of the summer night!
Where yonder woodbine creeps,
Fold, fold thy pinions light!
She sleeps!
My lady sleeps!
Sleeps!

Dreams of the summer night!
Tell her, her lover keeps
Watch! while in slumbers light
She sleeps!
My lady sleeps!
Sleeps!

— HENRY WADSWORTH
LONGFELLOW

44

To Daffodils

Fair Daffodils, we weep to see
  You haste away so soon:
As yet the early-rising sun
  Has not attained his noon.
    Stay, stay,
  Until the hasting day
    has run
  But to the evensong;
And, having prayed together, we
  Will go with you along.

We have short time to stay as you;
  We have as short a spring;
As quick a growth to meet decay,
  As you or anything.
    We die.
  As your hours do, and dry
    Away
  Like to the summer's rain;
Or as the pearls of morning's dew,
  Ne'er to be found again.

— ROBERT HERRICK

'Tis the Last Rose of Summer

'Tis the last rose of Summer,
  Left blooming alone;
All her lovely companions
  Are faded and gone;
No flower of her kindred,
  No rosebud is nigh,
To reflect back her blushes,
  Or give sigh for sigh!

I'll not leave thee, thou lone one,
  To pine on the stem;
Since the lovely are sleeping,
  Go sleep thou with them.
Thus kindly I scatter
  Thy leaves o'er the bed
Where thy mates of the garden
  Lie scentless and dead.

So soon may I follow,
  When friendships decay,
And from Love's shining circle
  The gems drop away!
When true hearts lie withered,

And fond ones are flown,
Oh! who would inhabit
This bleak world alone?

— THOMAS MOORE

Spring and Fall: To a Young Child

Márgarét, are you gríeving
Over Goldengrove unleaving?
Léaves, líke the things of man, you
With your fresh thoughts care for, can you?
Áh! ás the heart grows older
It will come to such sights colder
By and by, nor spare a sigh
Though worlds of wanwood leafmeal lie;
And yet you wíll weep and know why.
Now no matter, child, the name:
Sórrow's spríngs áre the same.
Nor mouth had, no nor mind, expressed
What heart heard of, ghost guessed:
It ís the blight man was born for,
It ís Margaret you mourn for.

— GERARD MANLEY HOPKINS

Weathers

This is the weather the cuckoo likes,
   And so do I;
When showers betumble the chestnut spikes,
   And nestlings fly:
And the little brown nightingale bills his
      best,
And they sit outside at "The Travellers'
      Rest,"
And maids come forth sprig-muslin drest,
And citizens dream of the south and west,
   And so do I.

This is the weather the shepherd shuns,
   And so do I;
When beeches drip in browns and duns,
   and thresh, and ply;
And hill-hid tides throb, throe on throe,
And meadow rivulets overflow,
And drops on gate-bars hang in a row,
And rooks in families homeward go,
   And so do I.

— THOMAS HARDY

To Autumn

Season of mists and mellow fruitfulness,
  Close bosom-friend of the maturing sun;
Conspiring with him how to load and bless
  With fruit the vines that round the thatch-
      eaves run;
To bend with apples the mossed cottage-
      trees,
  And fill all fruit with ripeness to the core;
    To swell the gourd, and plump the hazel
      shells
With a sweet kernel; to set budding more,
And still more, later flowers for the bees,
Until they think warm days will never
      cease,
    For summer has o'er-brimmed their
      clammy cells.

Who hath not seen thee oft amid thy store?
  Sometimes whoever seeks abroad may find
Thee sitting careless on a granary floor,
  Thy hair soft-lifted by the winnowing
      wind;
Or on a half-reaped furrow sound asleep,
  Drowsed with the fume of poppies, while
      thy hook

Spares the next swath and all its twinèd
   flowers:
And sometimes like a gleaner thou dost keep
   Steady thy laden head across a brook;
   Or by a cider-press, with patient look,
      Thou watchest the last oozings hours by
         hours.

Where are the songs of spring? Ay, where are
      they?
   Think not of them, thou hast thy music
         too,—
While barred clouds bloom the soft-dying
         day,
   And touch the stubble-plains with rosy
         hue;
Then in a wailful choir the small gnats mourn
   Among the river sallows, borne aloft
      Or sinking as the light wind lives or dies;
And full-grown lambs loud bleat from hilly
         bourn;
   Hedge-crickets sing; and now with treble
         soft

The redbreast whistles from a garden-
   croft;
And gathering swallows twitter in the
   skies.

— JOHN KEATS

Fall, Leaves, Fall

Fall, leaves, fall; die, flowers, away;
Lengthen night and shorten day;
Every leaf speaks bliss to me,
Fluttering from the autumn tree.
I shall smile when wreaths of snow
Blossom where the rose should grow;
I shall sing when night's decay
Ushers in a drearier day.

— EMILY BRONTË

Stopping by Woods on a Snowy Evening

Whose woods these are I think I know.
His house is in the village though;
He will not see me stopping here
To watch his woods fill up with snow.

My little horse must think it queer
To stop without a farmhouse near
Between the woods and frozen lake
The darkest evening of the year.

He gives his harness bells a shake
To ask if there is some mistake.
The only other sound's the sweep
Of easy wind and downy flake.

The woods are lovely, dark and deep.
But I have promises to keep,
And miles to go before I sleep,
And miles to go before I sleep.

— ROBERT FROST

Winter

When icicles hang by the wall,
   And Dick the shepherd blows his nail,
And Tom bears logs into the hall,
   And milk comes frozen home in pail;
When blood is nipped, and ways be foul,
Then nightly sings the staring owl.
Tu-whit, tu-who! a merry note,
While greasy Joan doth keel the pot.

When all aloud the wind doth blow,
   And coughing drowns the parson's saw,
And birds sit brooding in the snow,
   And Marian's nose looks red and raw,
When roasted crabs hiss in the bowl,
Then nightly sings the staring owl,
Tu-whit, tu-who! a merry note,
While greasy Joan doth keel the pot.

— WILLIAM SHAKESPEARE

Winter Portrait

A wrinkled, crabbed man they picture thee,
Old Winter, with a rugged beard as gray
As the long moss upon the apple tree;
Blue lipped, an ice drop at thy sharp blue
    nose,
Close muffled up, and on thy dreary way
Plodding alone through sleet and drifting
    snows.
They should have drawn thee by the high-
    leaped hearth,
Old Winter! seated in thy great armed chair,
Watching the children at their Christmas
    mirth.

— ROBERT SOUTHEY

The Ages of Man

At ten, a child; at twenty, wild;
   At thirty, tame if ever;
At forty, wise; at fifty, rich;
   At sixty, good or never.

— ANONYMOUS

The Snowstorm

Announced by all the trumpets of the sky,
Arrives the snow, and, driving o'er the fields,
Seems nowhere to alight: the whited air
Hides hills and woods, the river, and the
      heaven,
And veils the farmhouse at the garden's end.
The sled and traveler stopped, the courier's
      feet
Delayed, all friends shut out, the housemates
      sit
Around the radiant fireplace, enclosed
In a tumultuous privacy of storm.

  Come see the north wind's masonry.
Out of an unseen quarry evermore
Furnished with tile, the fierce artificer
Curves his white bastions with projected roof
Round every windward stake, or tree, or door.
Speeding, the myriad-handed, his wild work
So fanciful, so savage, nought cares he
For number or proportion. Mockingly,
On coop or kennel he hangs Parian wreaths;
A swan-like form invests the hidden thorn;
Fills up the farmer's lane from wall to wall,
Maugre the farmer's sighs; and, at the gate,

A tapering turret overtops the work.
And when his hours are numbered, and the
     world
Is all his own, retiring, as he were not,
Leaves, when the sun appears, astonished Art
To mimic in slow structures, stone by stone,
Built in an age, the mad wind's night-work,
The frolic architecture of the snow.

— RALPH WALDO EMERSON

Snowflakes

Out of the bosom of the air,
    Out of the cloud-folds of her garments
        shaken,
Over the woodlands brown and bare,
    Over the harvest-fields forsaken,
        Silent, and soft, and slow
        Descends the snow.

Even as our cloudy fancies take
    Suddenly shape in some divine expression,
Even as the troubled heart doth make

In the white countenance confession,
  The troubled sky reveals
  The grief it feels.

This is the poem of the air,
  Slowly in silent syllables recorded;
This is the secret of despair,
  Long in its cloudy bosom hoarded,
    Now whispered and revealed
    To wood and field.

— JOHN GREENLEAF WHITTIER

Woodman, Spare That Tree!

Woodman, spare that tree!
  Touch not a single bough!
In youth it shelter'd me,
  And I'll protect it now.

'Twas my forefather's hand
  That placed it near his cot;
There, woodman, let it stand,
  Thy axe shall harm it not!

That old familiar tree,
  Whose glory and renown
Are spread o'er land and sea—
  And would'st thou hew it down?
Woodman, forbear thy stroke!
  Cut not its earth-bound ties;
Oh, spare that aged oak,
  Now towering to the skies!

When but an idle boy,
  I sought its grateful shade;
In all their gushing joy
  Here, too, my sisters play'd.

My mother kiss'd me here;
  My father press'd my hand—
Forgive this foolish tear,
  But let that old oak stand!

My heart-strings round thee cling,
  Close as thy bark, old friend!
Here shall the wild bird sing,
  And still thy branches bend.
Old tree! the storm still brave!
  And, woodman, leave the spot;
While I've a hand to save,
  Thy axe shall harm it not!

— George P. Morris

58

Fog

The fog comes on little cat feet.
It sits looking over harbor and city,
On silent haunches and then moves on.

— CARL SANDBURG

The Fly

Busy, curious, thirsty fly,
Gently drink, and drink as I;
Freely welcome to my cup,
Could'st thou sip, and sip it up;
Make the most of life you may,
Life is short and wears away.

Just alike, both mine and thine,
Hasten quick to their decline;
Thine's a summer, mine's no more,
Though repeated to threescore;
Threescore summers when they're gone,
Will appear as short as one.

— WILLIAM OLDYS

On Aging

When you see me sitting quietly,
Like a sack left on the shelf,
Don't think I need your chattering.
I'm listening to myself.
Hold! Stop! Don't pity me!
Hold! Stop your sympathy!
Understanding if you got it,
Otherwise I'll do without it!

When my bones are stiff and aching
And my feet won't climb the stair,
I will only ask one favor:
Don't bring me no rocking chair.

When you see me walking, stumbling,
Don't study and get it wrong.
'Cause tired don't mean lazy
And every goodbye ain't gone.
I'm the same person I was back then,
A little less hair, a little less chin,
A lot less lungs and much less wind.
But ain't I lucky I can still breathe in.

— MAYA ANGELOU

Ode to a Nightingale

My heart aches, and a drowsy numbness
    pains
  My sense, as though of hemlock I had
    drunk,
Or emptied some dull opiate to the drains
  One minute past, and Lethe-wards had
    sunk:
'Tis not through envy of thy happy lot,
  But being too happy in thine happiness,—
    That thou, light-wingèd Dryad of the
      trees,
        In some melodious plot
  Of beechen green, and shadows
    numberless,
    Singest of summer in full-throated ease.

O for a draught of vintage! that hath been
  Cool'd a long age in the deep-delvèd earth,
Tasting of Flora and the country-green,
  Dance, and Provençal song, and sunburnt
    mirth!
O for a beaker full of the warm South,
  Full of the true, the blushful Hippocrene,
    With beaded bubbles winking at the brim,
      And purple-stainèd mouth;

That I might drink, and leave the world
　　unseen,
　　And with thee fade away into the forest
　　dim:

Fade far away, dissolve, and quite forget
　　What thou among the leaves hast never
　　　known,
The weariness, the fever, and the fret
　　Here, where men sit and hear each other
　　groan;
Where palsy shakes a few, sad, last gray hairs,
　　Where youth grows pale, and spectre-thin,
　　　and dies;
　　　Where but to think is to be full of sorrow
　　　And leaden-eyed despairs,
　　Where Beauty cannot keep her lustrous
　　eyes,
　　　Or new Love pine at them beyond
　　　tomorrow.

Away! away! for I will fly to thee,
　　Not charioted by Bacchus and his pards,
But on the viewless wings of Poesy,
　　Though the dull brain perplexes and
　　　retards:

Already with thee! tender is the night,
And haply the Queen Moon is on her
throne,
Clustered around by all her starry Fays;
But here there is no light,
Save what from heaven is with the breezes
blown
Through verdurous glooms and winding
mossy ways.

I cannot see what flowers are at my feet,
Nor what soft incense hangs upon the
boughs,
But, in embalmèd darkness, guess each sweet
Wherewith the seasonable month endows
The grass, the thicket, and the fruit-tree wild;
White hawthorn, and the pastoral
eglantine;
Fast fading violets covered up in leaves:
And mid-May's eldest child,
The coming musk-rose, full of dewy wine,
The murmurous haunt of flies on summer
eves.

Darkling I listen; and, for many a time
I have been half in love with easeful Death,

Call'd him soft names in many a musèd
      rhyme,
   To take into the air my quiet breath;
Now more than ever seems it rich to die,
   To cease upon the midnight with no pain,
      While thou art pouring forth thy soul
         abroad
         In such an ecstasy!
   Still wouldst thou sing, and I have ears in
         vain—
      To thy high requiem become a sod.

Thou wast not born for death, immortal Bird!
   No hungry generations tread thee down;
The voice I hear this passing night was heard
   In ancient days by emperor and clown:
Perhaps the self-same song that found a path
   Through the sad heart of Ruth, when, sick
      for home,
      She stood in tears amid the alien corn;
      The same that oft-times hath
   Charmed magic casements, opening on the
      foam
      Of perilous seas, in faery lands forlorn.

Forlorn! the very word is like a bell
   To toll me back from thee to my sole self!

Adieu! the fancy cannot cheat so well
  As she is famed to do, deceiving elf.
Adieu! adieu! thy plantive anthem fades
  Past the near meadows, over the still
      stream,
    Up the hill-side; and now 'tis buried
      deep
    In the next valley-glades:
Was it a vision, or a waking dream?
    Fled is that music:—do I wake or sleep?

— JOHN KEATS

A Bird Came Down the Walk

A Bird came down the Walk—
He did not know I saw—
He bit an Angleworm in halves
And ate the fellow, raw,

And then he drank a Dew
From a convenient Grass—
And then hopped sidewise to the Wall
To let a Beetle pass—

He glanced with rapid eyes
That hurried all around—
They looked like frightened Beads,
      I thought—
He stirred his Velvet Head

Like one in danger, Cautious,
I offered him a Crumb
And he unrolled his feathers
And rowed him softer home—

Than Oars divide the Ocean,
Too silver for a seam—
Or Butterflies, off Banks of Noon
Leap, plashless as they swim.

— EMILY DICKINSON

The Darkling Thrush

I leant upon a coppice gate
   When Frost was spectre-grey,
And Winter's dregs made desolate
   The weakening eye of day.
The tangled bine-stems scored the sky
   Like strings from broken lyres,
And all mankind that haunted nigh
   Had sought their household fires.

The land's sharp features seemed to be
   The Century's corpse outleant,
His crypt the cloudy canopy,
   The wind his death-lament.
The ancient pulse of germ and birth
   Was shrunken hard and dry,
And every spirit upon earth
   Seemed fervourless as I.

At once a voice arose among
   The bleak twigs overhead
In a full-hearted evensong
   Of joy illimited;

An agèd thrush, frail, gaunt, and small,
  In blast-beruffled plume,
Had chosen thus to fling his soul
  Upon the growing gloom.

So little cause for carolings
  Of such ecstatic sound
Was written on terrestrial things
  Afar or nigh around,
That I could think there trembled through
  His happy good-night air
Some blessed Hope, whereof he knew
  And I was unaware.

— THOMAS HARDY

The Tide Rises, the Tide Falls

The tide rises, the tide falls,
The twilight darkens, the curlew calls;
Along the sea-sands damp and brown
The traveller hastens toward the town,
  And the tide rises, the tide falls.

Darkness settles on roofs and walls,
But the sea, the sea in the darkness calls:
The little waves, with their soft, white hands,
Efface the footprints in the sands,
  And the tide rises, the tide falls.

The morning breaks; the steeds in their stalls
Stamp and neigh, as the hostler calls;
The day returns, but nevermore
Returns the traveller to the shore.
  And the tide rises, the tide falls.

— HENRY WADSWORTH
LONGFELLOW

The Marshes of Glynn

Glooms of the live-oaks, beautiful-braided
      and woven
With intricate shades of the vines that
      myriad-cloven
Clamber the forks of the multiform
      boughs,—

Emerald twilights,—
Virginal shy lights,
Wrought of the leaves to allure to the whisper
of vows,
When lovers pace timidly down through the
green colonnades
Of the dim sweet woods, of the dear dark
woods,
Of the heavenly woods and glades,
That run to the radiant marginal sand-beach
within
The wide sea-marshes of Glynn;—

Beautiful glooms, soft dusks in the noon-day
fire,—
Wildwood privacies, closets of lone desire,
Chamber from chamber parted with wavering
arras of leaves,—
Cells for the passionate pleasure of prayer to
the soul that grieves,
Pure with a sense of the passing of saints
through the wood.
Cool for the dutiful weighing of ill with
good;—

O braided dusks of the oak and woven shades
      of the vine,
While the riotous noon-day sun of the June-
      day long did shine
Ye held me fast in your heart and I held you
      fast in mine;
But now when the noon is no more, and riot
      is rest,
And the sun is a-wait at the ponderous gate of
      the West,
And the slant yellow beam down the wood-
      aisle doth seem
Like a lane into heaven that leads from a
      dream,—

Ay, now, when my soul all day hath drunken
      the soul of the oak,
And my heart is at ease from men, and the
      wearisome sound of the stroke
  Of the scythe of time and the trowel of
      trade is low,
  And belief overmasters doubt, and I know
      that I know,
And my spirit is grown to a lordly great
      compass within,

That the length and the breadth and the
    sweep of the marshes of Glynn
Will work me no fear like the fear they have
    wrought me of yore
When length was fatigue, and when breadth
    was but bitterness sore,
And when terror and shrinking and dreary
    unnamable pain
Drew over me out of the merciless miles of
    the plain,—
Oh, now, unafraid, I am fain to face
  The vast sweet visage of space.
To the edge of the wood I am drawn, I am
    drawn,
Where the gray beach glimmering runs, as a
    belt of the dawn,
  For a mete and a mark
    To the forest-dark:—
    So:
Affable live-oak, leaning low,—
Thus—with your favor—soft, with a reverent
    hand
(Not lightly touching your person, Lord of the
    land!),

Bending your beauty aside, with a step I
    stand
On the firm-packed sand,
    Free
By a world of marsh that borders a world of
    sea.
  Sinuous southward and sinuous northward
    the shimmering band
  Of the sand-beach fastens the fringe of the
    marsh to the folds of the land.
Inward and outward to northward and
    southward the beach-lines linger and
    curl
As a silver-wrought garment that clings to and
    follows the firm sweet limbs of a girl.
Vanishing, swerving, evermore curving again
    into sight,
Softly the sand-beach wavers away to a dim
    gray looping of light.
And what if behind me to westward the wall
    of the woods stands high?
The world lies east: how ample, the marsh
    and the sea and the sky!

A league and a league of marsh-grass, waist-
     high, broad in the blade,
Green, and all of a height, and unflecked with
     a light or a shade,
Stretch leisurely off, in a pleasant plain,
To the terminal blue of the main.

Oh, what is abroad in the marsh and the
     terminal sea?
Somehow my soul seems suddenly free
From the weighing of fate and the sad
     discussion of sin,
By the length and the breadth and the sweep
     of the marshes of Glynn.

Ye marshes, how candid and simple and
     nothing-withholding and free
Ye publish yourselves to the sky and offer
     yourselves to the sea!
Tolerant plains, that suffer the sea and the
     rains and the sun,
Ye spread and span like the catholic man who
     hath mightily won
God out of knowledge and good out of
     infinite pain
And sight out of blindness and purity out of a
     stain.

As the marsh-hen secretly builds on the
          watery sod,
Behold I will build me a nest on the
          greatness of God:
I will fly in the greatness of God as the
          marsh-hen flies
In the freedom that fills all the space 'twixt
          the marsh and the skies:

By so many roots as the marsh-grass sends in
          the sod
I will heartily lay me a-hold on the greatness
          of God:
Oh, like to the greatness of God is the
          greatness within
The range of the marshes, the liberal marshes
          of Glynn.

And the sea lends large, as the marsh: lo, out
          of his plenty the sea
Pours fast: full soon the time of the flood-tide
          must be:
Look how the grace of the sea doth go
About and about through the intricate
          channels that flow
     Here and there,
     Everywhere,

Till his waters have flooded the uttermost
        creeks and the low-lying lanes,
And the marsh is meshed with a million
        veins,
That like as with rosy and silvery essences
        flow
   In the rose-and-silver evening glow.
        Farewell, my lord Sun!
The creeks overflow: a thousand rivulets run
'Twixt the roots of the sod; the blades of the
        marsh-grass stir;
Passeth a hurrying sound of wings that
        westward whir;
Passeth, and all is still; and the currents cease
        to run;
And the sea and the marsh are one.

How still the plains of the waters be!
The tide is in his ecstasy.
The tide is at his highest height:
        And it is night.

And now from the Vast of the Lord will the
        waters of sleep
Roll in on the souls of men,

But who will reveal to our waking ken
The forms that swim and the shapes that
    creep
    Under the waters of sleep?

— S IDNEY   L ANIER

Silver Threads Among the Gold

Darling, I am growing old,
Silver threads among the gold.
Shine upon my brow today,
Life is fading fast away.
But, my darling, you will be
Always young and fair to me.

Yes, my darling you will be
Always young and fair to me.
Darling, I am growing old,
Silver threads among the gold,
Shine upon my brow today,
Life is fading fast away.

When your hair is silver white,
And your cheeks no longer bright,
With the roses of the May
I will kiss your lips and say:
Oh! my darling, mine alone, alone,
You have never older grown!
Yes, my darling, mine alone,
You have never older grown.

Always young and fair to me.
Darling, I am growing old,
Silver threads among the gold,
Shine upon my brow today,
Life is fading fast away.

Love can never more grow old,
Locks may lose their brown and gold;
Cheeks may fade and hollow grow,
But the hearts that love will know,
Never, never winter's frost and chill;
Summer warmth is in them still;
Never winter's frost and chill,
Summer warmth is in them still.

Always young and fair to me.
Darling, I am growing old,
Silver threads among the gold,
Shine upon my brow today,
Life is fading fast away.

— EBEN E. REXFORD

· T H R E E ·
Story Poems
and
Ballads

Sir Patrick Spence

The king sits in Dumferling toune,
   Drinking the blude-reid wine:
"O whar will I get guid sailor,
   To sail this schip of mine?"

Up and spak an eldern knicht,
   Sat at the kings richt kne:
"Sir Patrick Spence is the best sailor
   That sails upon the se."

The king has written a braid letter,
   And signed it wi his hand,
And sent it to Sir Patrick Spence,
   Was walking on the sand.

The first line that Sir Patrick red,
   A loud lauch lauched he;
The next line that Sir Patrick red,
   The teir blinded his e'e.

"O what is this has don this deid,
   This ill deid don to me,
To send me out this time o' the yeir
   To sail upon the se!

"Mak hast, mak hast, my mirry men all,
  Our guid schip sails the morne:"
"O say na sae, my master deir,
  For I feir a deadlie storme.

"Late late yestreen I saw the new moone,
  Wi' the auld moone in hir arme,
And I feir, I feir, my deir master.
  That we will cum to harme."

O our Scots nobles wer richt laith
  To weet their cork-heild schoone;
Bot lang owre a' the play wer playd,
  Thair hats they swam aboone.

O lang, lang may their ladies sit,
  Wi' thair fans into their hand,
Or eir they se Sir Patrick Spence
  Cum sailing to the land.

O lang, lang may the ladies stand,
  Wi thair gold kems in their hair,
Waiting for thair ain deir lords,
  For they'll se thame na mair.

Haf owre, haf owre to Aberdour,
  It's fiftie fadom deip,
And thair lies guid Sir Patrick Spence,
  Wi' the Scots lords at his feit.

— ANONYMOUS

Barbara Frietchie

[SEPTEMBER 13, 1862]

Up from the meadows rich with corn,
Clear in the cool September morn,

The clustered spires of Frederick stand
Green-walled by the hills of Maryland.

Round about them orchards sweep,
Apple and peach tree fruited deep,

Fair as the garden of the Lord
To the eyes of the famished rebel horde,

On that pleasant morn of the early fall
When Lee marched over the mountain-wall;

Over the mountains winding down,
Horse and foot, into Frederick town.

Forty flags with their silver stars,
Forty flags with their crimson bars,

Flapped in the morning wind: the sun
Of noon looked down, and saw not one.

Up rose old Barbara Frietchie then,
Bowed with her fourscore years and ten;

Bravest of all in Frederick town,
She took up the flag the men hauled down;

In her attic window the staff she set,
To show that one heart was loyal yet.

Up the street came the rebel tread,
Stonewall Jackson riding ahead.

Under his slouched hat left and right
He glanced; the old flag met his sight.

"Halt!"—the dust-brown ranks stood fast.
"Fire!"—out blazed the rifle-blast.

It shivered the window, pane and sash;
It rent the banner with seam and gash

Quick as it fell, from the broken staff
Dame Barbara snatched the silken scarf.

She leaned far out on the window-sill,
And shook it forth with a royal will.

"Shoot, if you must, this old gray head,
But spare your country's flag," she said.

A shade of sadness, a blush of shame,
Over the face of the leader came;

The nobler nature within him stirred
To life at that woman's deed and word;

"Who touches a hair of yon gray head
Dies like a dog! March on!" he said.

All day long through Frederick street
Sounded the tread of marching feet:

All day long that free flag tossed
Over the heads of the rebel host.

Ever its torn folds rose and fell
On the loyal winds that loved it well;

And through the hill-gaps sunset light
Shone over it with a warm good-night.

Barbara Frietchie's work is o'er,
And the Rebel rides on his raids no more.

Honor to her! and let a tear
Fall, for her sake, on Stonewall's bier.

Over Barbara Frietchie's grave,
Flag of Freedom and Union, wave!

Peace and order and beauty draw
Round thy symbol of light and law:

And ever the stars above look down
On thy stars below in Frederick town!

— JOHN GREENLEAF WHITTIER

La Belle Dame Sans Merci

O, what can ail thee, knight-at-arms,
  Alone and palely loitering?
The sedge has withered from the lake
  And no birds sing.

O, what can ail thee, knight-at-arms,
  So haggard, and so woe-begone?
The squirrel's granary is full,
  And the harvest's done.

I see a lily on thy brow,
  With anguish moist and fever dew;
And on thy cheeks a fading rose
  Fast withereth too.

I met a lady in the meads,
  Full beautiful—a faery's child,
Her hair was long, her foot was light
  And her eyes were wild.

I made a garland for her head,
  And bracelets too, and fragrant zone;
She look'd at me as she did love,
  And made sweet moan.

I set her on my pacing steed,
　And nothing else saw all day long,
For sidelong would she bend, and sing
　A faery's song.

She found me roots of relish sweet,
　And honey wild, and manna dew,
And sure in language strange she said—
　'I love thee true.'

She took me to her elfin grot,
　And there she wept, and sigh'd full sore,
And there I shut her wild wild eyes
　With kisses four.

And there she lullèd me asleep
　And there I dream'd—Ah! woe betide!
The latest dream I ever dream'd
　On the cold hillside.

I saw pale kings, and princes too,
　Pale warriors, death-pale were they all;
They cried—'La Belle Dame sans Merci
　Hath thee in thrall!'

I saw their starv'd lips in the gloam,
  With horrid warning gapèd wide,
And I awoke, and found me here
  On the cold hill's side.

And this is why I sojourn here,
  Alone and palely loitering,
Though the sedge is wither'd from the lake,
  And no birds sing.

— JOHN KEATS

The Raven

Once upon a midnight dreary, while I
      pondered, weak and weary,
Over many a quaint and curious volume of
      forgotten lore—
While I nodded, nearly napping, suddenly
      there came a tapping,
As of someone gently rapping, rapping at my
      chamber door.

" 'Tis some visitor," I muttered, "tapping at
      my chamber door—
            Only this and nothing more."

Ah, distinctly I remember it was in the bleak
      December;
And each separate dying ember wrought its
      ghost upon the floor.
Eagerly I wished the morrow;—vainly I had
      sought to borrow
From my books surcease of sorrow—sorrow
      for the lost Lenore—
For the rare and radiant maiden whom the
      angels name Lenore—
            Nameless *here* for evermore.

And the silken, sad, uncertain rustling of each
      purple curtain
Thrilled me—filled me with fantastic terrors
      never felt before;
So that now, to still the beating of my heart, I
      stood repeating
" 'Tis some visitor entreating entrance at my
      chamber door—
Some late visitor entreating entrance at my
      chamber door;—
            This it is and nothing more."

Presently my soul grew stronger; hesitating
    then no longer,
"Sir," said I, "or Madam, truly your
    forgiveness I implore;
But the fact is I was napping, and so gently
    you came rapping,
And so faintly you came tapping, tapping at
    my chamber door,
That I scarce was sure I heard you"—here I
    opened wide the door;
        Darkness there and nothing more.

Deep into that darkness peering, long I stood
    there wondering, fearing,
Doubting, dreaming dreams no mortal ever
    dared to dream before;
But the silence was unbroken, and the
    stillness gave no token,
And the only word there spoken was the
    whispered word, "Lenore!"
This I whispered, and an echo murmured
    back the word "Lenore!"
        Merely this and nothing more.

Back into the chamber turning, all my soul
    within me burning,

Soon again I heard a tapping somewhat
      louder than before.
"Surely," said I, "surely that is something at
      my window lattice;
Let me see, then, what thereat is, and this
      mystery explore—
Let my heart be still a moment and this
      mystery explore—
             'Tis the wind and nothing more!"

Open here I flung the shutter, when, with
      many a flirt and flutter
In there stepped a stately Raven of the saintly
      days of yore.
Not the least obeisance made he; not a
      minute stopped or stayed he;
But, with mien of lord or lady, perched above
      my chamber door—
Perched upon a bust of Pallas just above my
      chamber door—
             Perched, and sat, and nothing more

Then this ebony bird beguiling my sad fancy
      into smiling,
By the grave and stern decorum of the
      countenance it wore,

"Though thy crest be shorn and shaven,
      thou," I said, "art sure no craven,
Ghastly grim and ancient Raven wandering
      from the Nightly shore—
Tell me what thy lordly name is on the
      Night's Plutonian shore!"
            Quoth the Raven, "Nevermore."

Much I marvelled this ungainly fowl to hear
      discourse so plainly,
Though its answer little meaning, little
      relevancy, bore;
For we cannot help agreeing that no living
      human being
Ever yet was blessed with seeing bird above
      his chamber door—
Bird or beast upon the sculptured bust above
      his chamber door,
            With such name as "Nevermore."

But the Raven, sitting lonely on the placid
      bust, spoke only
That one word, as if his soul in that one word
      he did outpour.
Nothing farther then he uttered—not a
      feather then he fluttered—

Till I scarcely more than muttered, "Other
friends have flown before—
On the morrow *he* will leave me, as my hopes
have flown before."
Then the bird said, "Nevermore."

Startled at the stillness broken by reply so
aptly spoken,
"Doubtless," said I, "what it utters is its only
stock and store,
Caught from some unhappy master whom
unmerciful Disaster
Followed fast and followed faster till his
songs one burden bore—
Till the dirges of his hope that melancholy
burden bore
Of 'Never—nevermore.' "

But the Raven still beguiling all my fancy
into smiling,
Straight I wheeled a cushioned seat in front
of bird, and bust and door;
Then, upon the velvet sinking, I betook
myself to linking
Fancy unto fancy, thinking what this ominous
bird of yore—

What this grim, ungainly, ghastly, gaunt, and
      ominous bird of yore
          Meant in croaking "Nevermore!"

This I sat engaged in guessing, but no
      syllable expressing
To the fowl whose fiery eyes now burned into
      my bosom's core;
This and more I sat divining, with my head at
      ease reclining
On the cushion's velvet lining that the
      lamplight gloated o'er,
But whose velvet violet lining, with the
      lamplight gloating o'er,
          She shall press—ah! nevermore!

Then methought the air grew denser,
      perfumed from an unseen censer
Swung by seraphim, whose footfalls tinkled
      on the tufted floor.
"Wretch," I cried, "thy God hath lent thee,—
      by these angels he hath sent thee
Respite,—respite and nepenthe from the
      memories of Lenore!
Quaff, O, quaff this kind nepenthe, and forget
      this lost Lenore!"
          Quoth the Raven, "Nevermore!"

"Prophet!" said I, "thing of evil!—prophet
    still, if bird or devil!
Whether tempter sent, or whether tempest
    tossed thee here ashore,
Desolate yet all undaunted, on this desert
    land enchanted,—
On this home by Horror haunted,—tell me
    truly, I implore,—
Is there—*is* there balm in Gilead?—tell me,
    tell me, I implore!"
              Quoth the Raven, "Nevermore!"

"Prophet!" said I, "thing of evil!—prophet
    still, if bird or devil!
By that heaven that bends above us—by that
    God we both adore,
Tell this soul with sorrow laden, if, within the
    distant Aidenn,
It shall clasp a sainted maiden, whom the
    angels name Lenore,
Clasp a fair and radiant maiden, whom the
    angels name Lenore!"
              Quoth the Raven, "Nevermore!"

"Be that word our sign of parting, bird or
    fiend!" I shrieked, upstarting,—

"Get thee back into the tempest and the
        night's Plutonian shore!
Leave no black plume as a token of that lie
        thy soul hath spoken!
Leave my loneliness unbroken!—quit the
        bust above my door!
Take thy beak from out my heart, and take thy
        form from off my door!"
                Quoth the Raven, "Nevermore!"

And the Raven, never flitting, still is sitting,
        still is sitting
On the pallid bust of Pallas, just above my
        chamber door;
And his eyes have all the seeming of a
        demon's that is dreaming,
And the lamp-light o'er him streaming throws
        his shadow on the floor;
And my soul from out that shadow that lies
        floating on the floor
                Shall be lifted—nevermore!

— EDGAR ALLAN POE

The Ballad of the Oysterman

It was a tall young oysterman lived by the
    river-side,
His shop was just upon the bank, his boat was
    on the tide;
The daughter of a fisherman, that was so
    straight and slim,
Lived over on the other bank, right opposite
    to him.

It was the pensive oysterman that saw a
    lovely maid,
Upon a moonlight evening, a-sitting in the
    shade;
He saw her wave her handkerchief, as much
    as if to say,
'I 'm wide awake, young oysterman, and all
    the folks away.'

Then up arose the oysterman, and to himself
    said he,
'I guess I 'll leave the skiff at home, for fear
    that folks should see;
I read it in the story-book, that, for to kiss his
    dear,

Leander swam the Hellespont,—and I will
    swim this here.'

And he has leaped into the waves, and
    crossed the shining stream,
And he has clambered up the bank, all in the
    moonlight gleam;
Oh there were kisses sweet as dew, and
    words as soft as rain,—
But they have heard her father's step, and in
    he leaps again!

Out spoke the ancient fisherman,—'Oh, what
    was that, my daughter?'
' 'Twas nothing but a pebble, sir, I threw into
    the water.'
'And what is that, pray tell me, love, that
    paddles off so fast?'
'It 's nothing but a porpoise, sir, that's been
    a-swimming past.'

Out spoke the ancient fisherman,—'Now
    bring me my harpoon!
I'll get into my fishing-boat, and fix the fellow
    soon.'
Down fell that pretty innocent, as falls a
    snow-white lamb,

Her hair drooped round her pallid cheeks,
    like seaweed on a clam.

Alas for those two loving ones! she waked not
    from her swound,
And he was taken with the cramp, and in the
    waves was drowned;
But Fate has metamorphosed them, in pity of
    their woe,
And now they keep an oyster-shop for
    mermaids down below.

— OLIVER WENDELL HOLMES

The Charge of the Light Brigade

Half a league, half a league,
    Half a league onward,
All in the valley of Death
    Rode the six hundred.
"Forward, the Light Brigade!
Charge for the guns," he said:
Into the valley of Death
    Rode the six hundred.

"Forward, the Light Brigade!"
Was there a man dismay'd?
Not tho' the soldier knew
　　Someone had blunder'd:
Theirs not to make reply,
Theirs not to reason why,
Theirs but to do and die:
Into the valley of Death
　　Rode the six hundred.

Cannon to right of them,
Cannon to left of them,
Cannon in front of them
　　Volley'd and thunder'd;
Storm'd at with shot and shell,
Boldly they rode and well,
Into the jaws of Death,
Into the mouth of Hell
　　Rode the six hundred.

Flash'd all their sabers bare,
Flash'd as they turn'd in air
Sabring the gunners there,
Charging an army, while
　　All the world wonder'd:
Plung'd in the battery-smoke
Right thro' the line they broke;

Cossack and Russian
Reel'd from the saber-stroke
   Shatter'd and sunder'd.
Then they rode back, but not,
   Not the six hundred.

Cannon to right of them,
Cannon to left of them,
Cannon behind them
   Volley'd and thunder'd;
Storm'd at with shot and shell,
While horse and hero fell,
They that had fought so well
Came thro' the jaws of Death,
Back from the mouth of Hell,
All that was left of them,
   Left of six hundred.

When can their glory fade?
O the wild charge they made!
   All the world wonder'd.
Honor the charge they made!
Honor the Light Brigade,
   Noble six hundred!

— ALFRED, LORD TENNYSON

The Wreck of the Hesperus

It was the schooner Hesperus,
    That sailed the wintry sea;
And the skipper had taken his little daughter,
    To bear him company.

Blue were her eyes as the fairy-flax,
    Her cheeks like the dawn of day,
And her bosom white as the hawthorn buds,
    That ope in the month of May.

The skipper he stood beside the helm,
    His pipe was in his mouth,
And he watched how the veering flaw did
      blow
    The smoke now West, now South.

Then up and spake an old Sailòr,
    Had sailed to the Spanish Main,
"I pray thee, put into yonder port,
    For I fear a hurricane.

"Last night, the moon had a golden ring,
    And to-night no moon we see!"
The skipper, he blew a whiff from his pipe,
    And a scornful laugh laughed he.

Colder and louder blew the wind,
    A gale from the Northeast,
The snow fell hissing in the brine,
    And the billows frothed like yeast.

Down came the storm, and smote amain
    The vessel in its strength;
She shuddered and paused, like a frightened
      steed,
    Then leaped her cable's length.

"Come hither! come hither! my little
      daughter,
    And do not tremble so;
For I can weather the roughest gale
    That ever wind did blow."

He wrapped her warm in his seaman's coat
    Against the stinging blast;
He cut a rope from a broken spar,
    And bound her to the mast.

"O father! I hear the church-bells ring,
    Oh say, what may it be?"
" 'T is a fog-bell on a rock-bound coast!"—
    And he steered for the open sea.

"O father! I hear the sound of guns,
   Oh say, what may it be?"
"Some ship in distress, that cannot live
   In such an angry sea!"

"O father! I see a gleaming light,
   Oh say, what may it be?"
But the father answered never a word,
   A frozen corpse was he.

Lashed to the helm, all stiff and stark,
   With his face turned to the skies,
The lantern gleamed through the gleaming
      snow
   On his fixed and glassy eyes.

Then the maiden clasped her hands and
      prayed
   That savèd she might be;
And she thought of Christ, who stilled the
      wave,
   On the Lake of Galilee.

And fast through the midnight dark and drear,
   Through the whistling sleet and snow,
Like a sheeted ghost, the vessel swept
   Tow'rds the reef of Norman's Woe.

And ever the fitful gusts between
    A sound came from the land;
It was the sound of trampling surf
    On the rocks and the hard sea-sand.

The breakers were right beneath her bows,
    She drifted a dreary wreck,
And a whooping billow swept the crew
    Like icicles from her deck.

She struck where the white and fleecy waves
    Looked soft as carded wool,
But the cruel rocks, they gored her side
    Like the horns of an angry bull.

Her rattling shrouds, all sheathed in ice,
    With the masts went by the board;
Like a vessel of glass, she stove and sank,
    Ho! ho! the breakers roared!

At daybreak, on the bleak sea-beach,
    A fisherman stood aghast,
To see the form of a maiden fair,
    Lashed close to a drifting mast.

The salt sea was frozen on her breast,
    The salt tears in her eyes;

And he saw her hair, like the brown seaweed,
  On the billows fall and rise.

Such was the wreck of the Hesperus,
  In the midnight and the snow!
Christ save us all from a death like this,
  On the reef of Norman's Woe!

— HENRY WADSWORTH
  LONGFELLOW

The Shooting of Dan McGrew

A bunch of the boys were whooping it up in
    the Malamute saloon;
The kid that handles the music-box was
    hitting a jag-time tune;
Back of the bar, in a solo game, sat Dangerous
    Dan McGrew,
And watching his luck, was his light-o'-love,
    the lady that's known as Lou.

When out of the night, which was fifty below,
      and into the din and the glare,
There stumbled a miner fresh from the
      creeks, dog-dirty, and loaded for bear.
He looked like a man with a foot in the grave
      and scarcely the strength of a louse,
Yet he tilted a poke of dust on the bar, and he
      called for drinks for the house.
There was none could place the stranger's
      face, though we searched ourselves for
      a clue;
But we drank his health, and the last to drink
      was Dangerous Dan McGrew.

There's men that somehow just grip your
      eyes, and hold them hard like a spell;
And such was he, and he looked to me like a
      man who had lived in hell;
With a face most hair, and the dreary stare of
      a dog whose day is done,
As he watered the green stuff in his glass, and
      the drops fell one by one.
Then I got to figgering who he was, and
      wondering what he'd do,
And I turned my head—and there watching
      him was the lady that's known as Lou.

His eyes went rubbering round the room, and
     he seemed in a kind of daze,
Till at last that old piano fell in the way of his
     wandering gaze.
The rag-time kid was having a drink; there
     was no one else on the stool,
So the stranger stumbles across the room, and
     flops down there like a fool.
In a buckskin shirt that was glazed with dirt
     he sat, and I saw him sway;
Then he clutched the keys with his talon
     hands—my God! but that man could
     play.

Were you ever out in the Great Alone, when
     the moon was awful clear,
And the icy mountains hemmed you in with a
     silence you most could *hear;*
With only the howl of a timber wolf, and you
     camped there in the cold,
A half-dead thing in a stark, dead world,
     clean mad for the muck called gold;
While high overhead, green, yellow and red,
     the North Lights swept in bars?—
Then you've a hunch what the music meant
     . . . hunger and night and the stars.

And hunger not of the belly kind, that's
      banished with bacon and beans,
But the gnawing hunger of lonely men for a
      home and all that it means;
For a fireside far from the cares that are, four
      walls and a roof above;
But oh! so cramful of cosy joy, and crowned
      with a woman's love—
A woman dearer than all the world, and true
      as Heaven is true—
(God! how ghastly she looks through her
      rouge,—the lady that's known as Lou.)

Then on a sudden the music changed, so soft
      that you scarce could hear;
But you felt that your life had been looted
      clean of all that it once held dear;
That someone had stolen the woman you
      loved; that her love was a devil's lie;
That your guts were gone, and the best for
      you was to crawl away and die.
'Twas the crowning cry of a heart's
      despair, and it thrilled you through and
      through—
"I guess I'll make it a spread misere," said
      Dangerous Dan McGrew.

The music almost died away . . . then it burst
        like a pent-up flood;
And it seemed to say, "Repay, repay," and
        my eyes were blind with blood.
The thought came back of an ancient wrong,
        and it stung like a frozen lash,
And the lust awoke to kill, to kill . . . then the
        music stopped with a crash,
And the stranger turned, and his eyes they
        burned in a most peculiar way;
In a buckskin shirt that was glazed with dirt
        he sat, and I saw him sway;
Then his lips went in in a kind of grin, and he
        spoke, and his voice was calm,
And "Boys," says he, "you don't know me,
        and none of you care a damn;
But I want to state, and my words are straight,
        and I'll bet my poke they're true,
That one of you is a hound of hell . . . and that
        one is Dan McGrew."

Then I ducked my head, and the lights went
        out, and two guns blazed in the dark,
And a woman screamed, and the lights went
        up, and two men lay stiff and stark.
Pitched on his head, and pumped full of lead,
        was Dangerous Dan McGrew,

While the man from the creeks lay clutched
     to the breast of the lady that's known as
     Lou.

These are the simple facts of the case, and I
     guess I ought to know.
They say that the stranger was crazed with
     "hooch," and I'm not denying it's so.
I'm not so wise as the lawyer guys, but
     strictly between us two—
The woman that kissed him and—pinched
     his poke—was the lady that's known as
     Lou.

       — ROBERT W. SERVICE

Wynken, Blynken, and Nod

Wynken, Blynken, and Nod one night
    Sailed off in a wooden shoe,—
Sailed on a river of crystal light
    Into a sea of dew.

"Where are you going, and what do you
    wish?"
The old moon asked the three.
"We have come to fish for the herring-fish
    That live in this beautiful sea;
    Nets of silver and gold have we,"
        Said Wynken,
        Blynken,
        And Nod.

The old moon laughed and sang a song,
    As they rocked in the wooden shoe;
And the wind that sped them all night long
    Ruffled the waves of dew;
The little stars were the herring-fish
    That lived in the beautiful sea.
"Now cast your nets wherever you wish,—
    Never afeard are we!"
    So cried the stars to the fishermen three,
        Wynken,
        Blynken,
        And Nod.

All night long their nets they threw
    To the stars in the twinkling foam,—
Then down from the skies came the wooden
        shoe,

Bringing the fishermen home:
'Twas all so pretty a sail, it seemed
  As if it could not be;
And some folk thought 'twas a dream they'd
    dreamed
  Of sailing that beautiful sea;
  But I shall name you the fishermen three:
      Wynken,
      Blynken,
      And Nod.

Wynken and Blynken are two little eyes,
  And Nod is a little head,
And the wooden shoe that sailed the skies
  Is a wee one's trundle-bed;
So shut your eyes while Mother sings
  Of wonderful sights that be,
And you shall see the beautiful things
  As you rock on the misty sea
  Where the old shoe rocked the fishermen
    three,—
      Wynken,
      Blynken,
      And Nod.

— EUGENE FIELD

Aiken Drum

There was a man lived in the moon,
  and his name was Aiken Drum.
And he played upon a ladle,
  and his name was Aiken Drum.

And his hat was made of good cream cheese,
  and his name was Aiken Drum.
And he played upon a ladle, etc.

And his coat was made of good roast beef,
  and his name was Aiken Drum.

And his buttons were made of penny loaves,
  and his name was Aiken Drum.

His waistcoat was made of crust of pies,
  and his name was Aiken Drum.

His breeches were made of haggis bags,
  and his name was Aiken Drum.

There was a man in another town,
  and his name was Willy Wood;
And he played upon a razor,
  and his name was Willy Wood.

And he ate up all the good cream cheese,
    and his name was Willy Wood.
And he played upon a razor, etc.

And he ate up all the good roast beef,
    and his name was Willy Wood.

And he ate up all the penny loaves,
    and his name was Willy Wood.

And he ate up all the good pie crust,
    and his name was Willy Wood.

But he choked upon the haggis bags,
    and there was an end of Willy Wood.
And he played upon a razor,
    and his name was Willy Wood.

— ANONYMOUS

118

The Walrus and the Carpenter

The sun was shining on the sea,
   Shining with all his might:
He did his very best to make
   The billows smooth and bright—
And this was odd, because it was
   The middle of the night.

The moon was shining sulkily,
   Because she thought the sun
Had got no business to be there
   After the day was done—
"It's very rude of him," she said,
   "To come and spoil the fun!"

The sea was wet as wet could be,
   The sands were dry as dry.
You could not see a cloud, because
   No cloud was in the sky:
No birds were flying overhead—
   There were no birds to fly.

The Walrus and the Carpenter
   Were walking close at hand:
They wept like anything to see
   Such quantities of sand.

"If this were only cleared away,"
    They said, "it *would* be grand!"

"If seven maids with seven mops
    Swept it for half a year,
Do you suppose," the Walrus said,
    "That they could get it clear?"
"I doubt it," said the Carpenter,
    And shed a bitter tear.

"O Oysters, come and walk with us!"
    The Walrus did beseech.
"A pleasant walk, a pleasant talk,
    Along the briny beach:
We cannot do with more than four,
    To give a hand to each."

The eldest Oyster looked at him,
    But never a word he said:
The eldest Oyster winked his eye,
    And shook his heavy head—
Meaning to say he did not choose
    To leave the oyster-bed.

But four young Oysters hurried up,
    All eager for the treat:
Their coats were brushed, their faces washed,

Their shoes were clean and neat—
And this was odd, because, you know,
    They hadn't any feet.

Four other Oysters followed them,
    And yet another four;
And thick and fast they came at last,
    And more, and more, and more—
All hopping through the frothy waves,
    And scrambling to the shore.

The Walrus and the Carpenter
    Walked on a mile or so,
And then they rested on a rock
    Conveniently low:
And all the little Oysters stood
    And waited in a row.

"The time has come," the Walrus said,
    "To talk of many things:
Of shoes—and ships—and sealing-wax—
    Of cabbages—and kings—
And why the sea is boiling hot—
    And whether pigs have wings."

"But wait a bit," the Oysters cried,
    "Before we have our chat;

For some of us are out of breath,
    And all of us are fat!"
"No hurry!" said the Carpenter.
    They thanked him much for that.

"A loaf of bread," the Walrus said,
    "Is what we chiefly need:
Pepper and vinegar besides
    Are very good indeed—
Now, if you're ready, Oysters dear,
    We can begin to feed."

"But not on us!" the Oysters cried,
    Turning a little blue.
"After such kindness, that would be
    A dismal thing to do!"
"The night is fine," the Walrus said,
    "Do you admire the view?

"It was so kind of you to come!
    And you are very nice!"
The Carpenter said nothing but
    "Cut us another slice.
I wish you were not quite so deaf—
    I've had to ask you twice!"

"It seems a shame," the Walrus said,
  "To play them such a trick,
After we've brought them out so far,
  And made them trot so quick!"
The Carpenter said nothing but
  "The butter's spread too thick!"

"I weep for you," the Walrus said:
  "I deeply sympathize."
With sobs and tears he sorted out
  Those of the largest size,
Holding his pocket-handkerchief
  Before his streaming eyes.

"O Oysters," said the Carpenter,
  "You've had a pleasant run!
Shall we be trotting home again?"
  But answer came there none—
And this was scarcely odd, because
  They'd eaten every one.

— LEWIS CARROLL

Greensleeves

Greensleeves was all my joy,
  Greensleeves was my delight;
Greensleeves was my heart of gold,
  And who but Lady Greensleeves.

Alas, my Love! ye do me wrong
  To cast me off discourteously;
And I have loved you so long,
  Delighting in your company.

I have been ready at your hand,
  To grant whatever you would crave:
I have both waged life and land,
  Your love and goodwill for to have.

I bought thee kerchers to thy head,
  That were wrought fine and gallantly;
I kept thee both at board and bed,
  Which cost my purse well favouredly.

I bought thee petticoats of the best,
  The cloth so fine as fine might be;

I gave thee jewels for thy chest,
    And all this cost I spent on thee.

Thy purse and eke thy gay gilt knives,
    Thy pincase gallant to the eye;
No better wore the burgess wives,
    And yet thou wouldst not love me.

Thy gown was of the grassy green,
    Thy sleeves of satin hanging by,
Which made thee be our harvest queen,
    And yet thou wouldst not love me.

My gayest gelding I thee gave,
    To ride wherever liked thee;
No lady ever was so brave,
    And yet thou wouldst not love me.

My men were clothed all in green,
    And they did ever wait on thee;
All this was gallant to be seen,
    And yet thou wouldst not love me.

For every morning when thou rose,
    I sent thee dainties orderly,
To cheer thy stomach from all woes,
    And yet thou wouldst not love me.

Well, I will pray to God on high,
   That thou my constancy mayst see,
And that yet once before I die,
   Thou wilt vouchsafe to love me.

Greensleeves, now farewell! adieu!
   God I pray to prosper thee;
For I am still thy lover true.
   Come once again and love me.

Greensleeves was all my joy,
   Greensleeves was my delight;
Greensleeves was my heart of gold,
   And who but Lady Greensleeves.

— ANONYMOUS

· *F O U R* ·

Families
and
Children

I Remember, I Remember

I remember, I remember,
  The house where I was born,
The little window where the sun
  Came peeping in at morn:
He never came a wink too soon,
  Nor brought too long a day;
But now, I often wish the night
  Had borne my breath away.

I remember, I remember,
  The roses, red and white;
The violets and the lily-cups,
  Those flowers made of light!
The lilacs where the robin built,
  And where my brother set
The laburnum on his birthday,—
  The tree is living yet!

I remember, I remember,
  Where I was used to swing;
And thought the air must rush as fresh
  To swallows on the wing:
My spirit flew in feathers then,
  That is so heavy now,

And summer pools could hardly cool
   The fever on my brow!

I remember, I remember,
   The fir trees dark and high;
I used to think their slender tops
   Were close against the sky:
It was a childish ignorance,
   But now 'tis little joy
To know I'm farther off from heaven
   Than when I was a boy.

— THOMAS HOOD

"Introduction" to Songs of Innocence

Piping down the valleys wild,
Piping songs of pleasant glee,
On a cloud I saw a child,
And he laughing said to me:

"Pipe a song about a Lamb."
So I piped with merry cheer.
"Piper, pipe that song again."
So I piped; he wept to hear.

"Drop thy pipe, thy happy pipe;
Sing thy songs of happy cheer."
So I sung the same again
While he wept with joy to hear.

"Piper, sit thee down and write
In a book that all may read."
So he vanished from my sight,
And I plucked a hollow reed,

And I made a rural pen,
And I stained the water clear,
And I wrote my happy songs
Every child may joy to hear.

— WILLIAM BLAKE

Home, Sweet Home

'Mid pleasures and palaces though we may
    roam,
Be it ever so humble, there's no place like
    home;
A charm from the sky seems to hallow us
    there,

Which, seek through the world, is ne'er met
    with elsewhere.
  Home, home, sweet, sweet home!
There's no place like home, oh, there's no
    place like home!

An exile from home, splendor dazzles in vain;
Oh, give me my lowly thatched cottage again!
The birds singing gayly, that came at my
    call—
Give me them—and the peace of mind,
    dearer than all!
  Home, home, sweet, sweet home!
There's no place like home, oh, there's no
    place like home!

I gaze on the moon as I tread the drear wild,
And feel that my mother now thinks of her
    child,
As she looks on that moon from our own
    cottage door
Thro' the woodbine, whose fragrance shall
    cheer me no more.
  Home, home, sweet, sweet home!
There's no place like home, oh, there's no
    place like home!

How sweet 'tis to sit 'neath a fond father's
  smile,
And the caress of a mother to soothe and
  beguile!
Let others delight 'mid new pleasure to roam,
But give me, oh, give me, the pleasures of
  home,
 Home, home, sweet, sweet home!
There's no place like home, oh, there's no
  place like home!

To thee I'll return, overburdened with care;
The heart's dearest solace will smile on me
  there;
No more from that cottage again will I roam;
Be it ever so humble, there's no place like
  home.
 Home, home, sweet, sweet home!
There's no place like home, oh, there's no
  place like home!

— JOHN HOWARD PAYNE

133

When Mother Reads Aloud

"When mother reads aloud the past
Seems real as every day;
I hear the tramp of armies vast,
I see the spears and lances cast,
I join the thrilling fray;
Brave knights and ladies fair and proud
I meet when mother reads aloud.

"When mother reads aloud, far lands
Seem very near and true;
I cross the desert's gleaming sands,
Or hunt the jungle's prowling bands,
Or sail the ocean blue;
Far heights, whose peaks the cold mists
      shroud,
I scale, when mother reads aloud.

"When mother reads aloud I long
For noble deeds to do—
To help the right, redress the wrong,
It seems so easy to be strong, so simple to be
      true,
O, thick and fast the visions crowd
When mother reads aloud."

— ANONYMOUS

To My Dear and Loving Husband

If ever two were one, then surely we.
If ever man were loved by wife, then thee;
If ever wife was happy in a man,
Compare with me, ye women, if you can.
I prize thy love more than whole mines of
      gold
Or all the riches that the East doth hold.
My love is such that rivers cannot quench,
Nor ought but love from thee, give
      recompense.
Thy love is such I can no way repay,
The heavens reward thee manifold, I pray.
Then while we live, in love let's so persevere
That when we live no more, we may live
      ever.

— ANNE BRADSTREET

Mother o' Mine

If I were hanged on the highest hill,
   Mother o' mine, O mother o' mine!
I know whose love would follow me still,
   Mother o' mine, O mother o' mine!
If I were drowned in the deepest sea,
   Mother o' mine, O mother o' mine!
I know whose tears would come down to me,
   Mother o' mine, O mother o' mine!
If I were damned by body and soul,
I know whose prayers would make me whole,
   Mother o' mine, O mother o' mine!

— RUDYARD KIPLING

A Visit from Saint Nicholas

'Twas the night before Christmas, when all
     through the house
Not a creature was stirring, not even a mouse;
The stockings were hung by the chimney
     with care,
In hopes that St. Nicholas soon would be
     there;

The children were nestled all snug in their
 beds,
While visions of sugar-plums danced in their
 heads;
And mamma in her kerchief, and I in my cap,
Had just settled our brains for a long winter's
 nap,
When out on the lawn there arose such a
 clatter,
I sprang from the bed to see what was the
 matter.
Away to the window I flew like a flash,
Tore open the shutters, and threw up the
 sash.
The moon on the breast of the new-fallen
 snow
Gave a luster of mid-day to objects below,
When, what to my wondering eyes should
 appear,
But a miniature sleigh, and eight tiny
 reindeer,
With a little old driver, so lively and quick,
I knew in a moment it must be St. Nick.
More rapid than eagles his coursers they
 came,
And he whistled, and shouted, and called
 them by name;

"Now, *Dasher!* now, *Dancer!* now, *Prancer*
    and *Vixen!*
On, *Comet!* on, *Cupid!* on, *Dunder* and
    Blitzen!
To the top of the porch! To the top of the
    wall!
Now, dash away! Dash away! Dash away all!"
As dry leaves that before the wild hurricane
    fly,
When they meet with an obstacle, mount to
    the sky;
So up to the housetop the coursers they flew,
With the sleigh full of toys, and St. Nicholas,
    too.
And then in a twinkling, I heard on the roof
The prancing and pawing of each little hoof.
As I drew in my head, and was turning
    around,
Down the chimney St. Nicholas came with a
    bound.
He was dressed all in fur, from his head to his
    foot,
And his clothes were all tarnished with ashes
    and soot;
A bundle of toys he had flung on his back,
And he looked like a peddler just opening his
    pack.

His eyes—how they twinkled!—his dimples
how merry!
His cheeks were like roses, his nose like a
cherry!
His droll little mouth was drawn up like a
bow,
And the beard of his chin was as white as the
snow;
The stump of a pipe he held tight in his teeth,
And the smoke it encircled his head like a
wreath;
He had a broad face and a round little belly,
That shook when he laughed like a bowlful of
jelly.
He was chubby and plump, a right jolly old
elf,
And I laughed when I saw him, in spite of
myself;
A wink of his eye and a twist of his head,
Soon gave me to know I had nothing to
dread;
He spoke not a word, but went straight to his
work,
And filled all the stockings; then turned with
a jerk,
And laying his finger aside of his nose,
And giving a nod, up the chimney he rose;

He sprang to his sleigh, to his team gave a
      whistle,
And away they all flew like the down of a
      thistle;
But I heard him exclaim, ere he drove out of
      sight,
*"Happy Christmas to all, and to all a good
      night!"*

— CLEMENT MOORE

The Children's Hour

Between the dark and the daylight,
   When the night is beginning to lower,
Comes a pause in the day's occupations,
   That is known as the Children's Hour.

I hear in the chamber above me
   The patter of little feet,
The sound of a door that is opened,
   And voices soft and sweet.

From my study I see in the lamplight,
   Descending the broad hall stair,

Grave Alice, and laughing Allegra,
　And Edith with golden hair.

A whisper, and then a silence:
　Yet I know by their merry eyes
They are plotting and planning together
　To take me by surprise.

A sudden rush from the stairway,
　A sudden raid from the hall!
By three doors left unguarded
　They enter my castle wall!

They climb up into my turret
　O'er the arms and back of my chair;
If I try to escape, they surround me;
　They seem to be everywhere.

They almost devour me with kisses,
　Their arms about me entwine,
Till I think of the Bishop of Bingen
　In his Mouse-Tower on the Rhine!

Do you think, O blue-eyed banditti,
　Because you have scaled the wall,
Such an old mustache as I am
　Is not a match for you all!

I have you fast in my fortress,
    And will not let you depart,
But put you down into the dungeon
    In the round-tower of my heart.

And there will I keep you forever,
    Yes, forever and a day,
Till the walls shall crumble to ruin,
    And moulder in dust away.

— HENRY WADSWORTH
LONGFELLOW

Children

Monday's child is fair of face,
Tuesday's child is full of grace,
Wednesday's child is full of woe,
Thursday's child has far to go,
Friday's child is loving and giving,
Saturday's child works hard for his living,
And the child that is born on the Sabbath day
Is bonny and blithe, and good and gay.

— ANONYMOUS

Here We Come a-Wassailing

Here we come a-wassailing
Among the leaves so green;
Here we come a wand'ring,
So fair to be seen.
Refrain:
Love and joy come to you,
And to you your wassail too;
And God bless you and send you
A Happy New Year,
And God send you a Happy New Year.

We are not daily beggars
That beg from door to door;
But we are neighbors' children,
Whom you have seen before.

God bless the master of this house,
Likewise the mistress too;
And all the little children,
That round the table go.

And all your kin and kinsfolk
That dwell both far and near,
We wish a Merry Christmas
And a Happy New Year.

— ANONYMOUS

The Sugar-Plum Tree

Have you ever heard of the Sugar-Plum Tree?
   'Tis a marvel of great renown!
It blooms on the shore of the Lollipop sea
   In the garden of Shut-Eye Town;
The fruit that it bears is so wondrously sweet
   (As those who have tasted it say)
That good little children have only to eat
   Of that fruit to be happy next day.

When you've got to the tree, you would have
      a hard time
   To capture the fruit which I sing;
The tree is so tall that no person could climb
   To the boughs where the sugar-plums
      swing!
But up in that tree sits a chocolate cat,
   And a gingerbread dog prowls below—
And this is the way you contrive to get at
   Those sugar-plums tempting you so:

You say but the word to that gingerbread dog
   And he barks with such terrible zest
That the chocolate cat is at once all agog,
   As her swelling proportions attest.

And the chocolate cat goes cavorting around
   From this leafy limb unto that,
And the sugar-plums tumble, of course, to the
      ground—
   Hurrah for that chocolate cat!

There are marshmallows, gumdrops, and
      peppermint canes,
   With stripings of scarlet or gold,
And you carry away of the treasure that rains
   As much as your apron can hold!
So come, little child, cuddle closer to me
   In your dainty white nightcap and gown,
And I'll rock you away to that Sugar-Plum
      Tree
   In the garden of Shut-Eye Town.

— EUGENE FIELD

There Was a Little Girl

There was a little girl, she had a little curl
  Right in the middle of her forehead;
And when she was good, she was very, very
    good,
  And when she was bad, she was horrid.

— HENRY WADSWORTH
LONGFELLOW

Cradle Song

[FROM THE GERMAN]

Sleep, baby, sleep!
Thy father's watching the sheep,
Thy mother's shaking the dreamland tree,
And down drops a little dream for thee.
Sleep, baby, sleep!

Sleep, baby, sleep!
The large stars are the sheep,
The little stars are the lambs, I guess,
The bright moon is the shepherdess.
Sleep, baby, sleep!

Sleep, baby, sleep!
And cry not like a sheep.
Else the sheep-dog will bark and whine,
And bite this naughty child of mine.
Sleep, baby, sleep!

Sleep, baby, sleep!
Thy Saviour loves His sheep;
He is the Lamb of God on high
Who for our sakes came down to die.
Sleep, baby, sleep!

Sleep, baby, sleep!
Away to tend the sheep,
Away, thou sheep-dog fierce and wild,
And do not harm my sleeping child!
Sleep, baby, sleep!

— ELIZABETH PRENTISS

How's My Boy?

"Ho, sailor of the sea!
How's my boy—my boy?"
"What's your boy's name, good wife,
And in what good ship sailed he?"

"My boy John—
He that went to sea—
What care I for the ship, sailor?
My boy's my boy to me.

"You come back from sea,
And not know my John?
I might as well have ask'd some landsman
Yonder down in the town.

There's not an ass in all the parish
But knows my John

"How's my boy—my boy?
And unless you let me know,
I'll swear you are no sailor,
Blue jacket or no,
Brass buttons or no, sailor,
Anchor and crown or no!
Sure his ship was the 'Jolly Briton' "—
"Speak low, woman, speak low!"

"And why should I speak low, sailor,
About my own boy John?
If I was loud as I am proud
I'd sing him over the town!
Why should I speak low, sailor?"
"That good ship went down."

"How's my boy—my boy?
What care I for the ship, sailor,
I was never aboard her?
Be she afloat or be she aground,
Sinking or swimming, I'll be bound
Her owners can afford her!
I say, how's my John?"

"Every man on board went down,
Every man aboard her."
"How's my boy—my boy?
What care I for the men, sailor?
I'm not their mother—
How's my boy—my boy?
Tell me of him and no other!
How's my boy—my boy?"

— SYDNEY DOBELL

The Pied Piper of Hamelin

I

Hamelin Town's in Brunswick,
    By famous Hanover city;
The river Weser, deep and wide,
Washes its wall on the southern side;
A pleasanter spot you never spied;
    But, when begins my ditty,
Almost five hundred years ago,
To see the townsfolk suffer so
    From vermin, was a pity.

Rats!
They fought the dogs and killed the cats,
   And bit the babies in the cradles,
And ate the cheeses out of the vats,
   And licked the soup from the cook's own
      ladles,
Split open the kegs of salted sprats,
Made nests inside men's Sunday hats,
And even spoiled the women's chats
     By drowning their speaking
     With shrieking and squeaking.
In fifty different sharps and flats.

I I I

At last the people in a body
   To the Town Hall came flocking:
" 'Tis clear," cried they, "our Mayor's a
     noddy;
And as for our corporation—shocking
To think we buy gowns lined with ermine
For dolts that can't or won't determine
What's best to rid us of our vermin!
You hope, because you're old and obese,
To find in the furry civic robe ease?
Rouse up, Sirs! Give your brains a racking

151

To find the remedy we're lacking,
Or, sure as fate, we'll send you packing!"
At this the Mayor and Corporation
Quaked with a mighty consternation.

An hour they sat in council,
    At length the Mayor broke silence:
"For a guilder I'd my ermine gown sell,
    I wish I were a mile hence!
It's easy to bid one rack one's brain—
I'm sure my poor head aches again
I've scratched it so, and all in vain.
Oh for a trap, a trap, a trap!"
Just as he said this, what should hap
At the chamber door but a gentle tap?
"Bless us," cried the Mayor, "what's that?"
(With the Corporation as he sat,
Looking little though wondrous fat;
Nor brighter was his eye, nor moister
Than a too-long-opened oyster,
Save when at noon his paunch grew mutinous
For a plate of turtle green and glutinous.)
"Only a scraping of shoes on the mat?
Anything like the sound of a rat
Makes my heart go pit-a-pat!"

"Come in!"—the Mayor cried, looking
      bigger:
And in did come the strangest figure!
His queer long coat from heel to head
Was half of yellow and half of red,
And he himself was tall and thin,
With sharp blue eyes, each like a pin,
And light loose hair, yet swarthy skin,
No tuft on cheek nor beard on chin,
But lips where smiles went out and in;
There was no guessing his kith and kin:
And nobody could enough admire
The tall man and his quaint attire.
Quoth one: "It's as my great-grandsire,
Starting up at the Trump of Doom's tone,
Had walked this way from his painted
      tombstone!"

He advanced to the council-table:
And, "Please your honours," said he, "I'm
      able,
By means of a secret charm, to draw

All creatures living beneath the sun,
That creep or swim or fly or run,
After me so as you never saw!
And I chiefly use my charm
On creatures that do people harm,
The mole and toad and newt and viper;
And people called me the Pied Piper."
(And here they noticed round his neck
A scarf of red and yellow stripe,
To match with his coat of the self-same
cheque;
And at the scarf's end hung a pipe;
And his fingers, they noticed, were ever
straying
As if impatient to be playing
Upon this pipe, as low it dangled
Over his vesture so old-fangled.)
"Yet," said he, "poor piper as I am,
In Tartary I freed the Cham,
Last June, from his huge swarm of gnats;
I eased in Asia the Nizam
Of a monstrous brood of vampyre-bats:
And as for what your brain bewilders,
If I can rid your town of rats
Will you give me a thousand guilders?"
"One? fifty thousand!"—was the exclamation
Of the astonished Mayor and Corporation.

Into the street the Piper stept,
   Smiling first a little smile,
As if he knew what magic slept
   In his quiet pipe the while;
Then, like a musical adept,
To blow the pipe his lips he wrinkled,
And green and blue his sharp eyes twinkled
Like a candle-flame where salt is sprinkled;
And ere three shrill notes the pipe uttered,
You heard as if an army muttered;
And the muttering grew to a grumbling;
And the grumbling grew to a mighty
      rumbling;
And out of the houses the rats came tumbling.
Great rats, small rats, lean rats, brawny rats,
Brown rats, black rats, grey rats, tawny rats,
Grave old plodders, gay young friskers,
   Fathers, mothers, uncles, cousins,
Cocking tails and pricking whiskers,
   Families by ten and dozens,
Brothers, sisters, husbands, wives—
Followed the Piper for their lives.
From street to street he piped advancing,
And step for step they followed dancing,
Until they came to the river Weser
   Wherein all plunged and perished!

—Save one who, stout as Julius Caesar,
Swam across and lived to carry
  (As he, the manuscript he cherished)
To Rat-land home his commentary:
Which was, "At the first shrill notes of the
        pipe,
I heard a sound as of scraping tripe,
And putting apples, wondrous ripe,
Into a cider-press's gripe:
And a moving away of pickle-tub-boards,
And a leaving ajar of conserve-cupboards,
And a drawing the corks of train-oil flasks,
And a breaking the hoops of butter-casks:
And it seemed as if a voice
  (Sweeter far than by harp or by psaltery
Is breathed) called out, 'Oh rats, rejoice!
  The world is grown to one vast drysaltery!
So munch on, crunch on, take your nuncheon,
Breakfast, supper, dinner, luncheon!'
And just as a bulky sugar-puncheon,
All ready staved, like a great sun shone
Glorious scarce an inch before me,
Just as methought it said, 'Come, bore me!'
—I found the Weser rolling o'er me."

VIII

You should have heard the Hamelin people
Ringing the bells till they rocked the steeple.
"Go," cried the Mayor, "and get long poles!
Poke out the nests and block up the holes!
Consult with carpenters and builders,
And leave in our town not even a trace
Of the rats!"—when suddenly, up the face
Of the Piper perked in the market-place,
With a, "First, if you please, my thousand
      guilders!"

IX

A thousand guilders! The Mayor looked blue;
So did the Corporation too.
For council dinners made rare havoc
With Claret, Moselle, Vin-de-Grave, Hock;
And half the money would replenish
Their cellar's biggest butt with Rhenish.
To pay this sum to a wandering fellow
With a gipsy coat of red and yellow!
"Beside," quoth the Mayor with a knowing
      wink,
"Our business was done at the river's brink;
We saw with our eyes the vermin sink,
And what's dead can't come to life, I think.

So, friend, we're not the folks to shrink
From the duty of giving you something for
        drink,
And a matter of money to put in your poke;
But as for the guilders, what we spoke
Of them, as you very well know, was in joke.
Beside, our losses have made us thrifty.
A thousand guilders! Come, take fifty!"

X

The Piper's face fell, and he cried
"No trifling! I can't wait, beside!
I've promised to visit by dinner time
Bagdat, and accept the prime
Of the Head-Cook's pottage, all he's rich in,
For having left, in the Caliph's kitchen,
Of a nest of scorpions no survivor:
With him I proved no bargain-driver,
With you, don't think I'll bate a stiver!
And folks who put me in a passion
May find me pipe after another fashion."

XI

"How?" cried the Mayor, "d'ye think I brook
Being worse treated than a Cook?

Insulted by a lazy ribald
With idle pipe and vesture piebald?
You threaten us, fellow? Do your worst,
Blow your pipe there till you burst!"

XII

Once more he stept into the street;
  And to his lips again
  Laid his long pipe of smooth straight cane;
And ere he blew three notes (such sweet
Soft notes as yet musician's cunning
  Never gave the enraptured air)
There was a rustling that seemed like a
            bustling
Of merry crowds justling at pitching and
            hustling,
Small feet were pattering, wooden shoes
            clattering,
Little hands clapping and little tongues
            chattering,
And, like fowls in a farm-yard when barley is
            scattering,
Out came the children running.
All the little boys and girls,
With rosy cheeks and flaxen curls,
And sparkling eyes and teeth like pearls,

Tripping and skipping, ran merrily after
The wonderful music with shouting and
  laughter.

The Mayor was dumb, and the Council stood
As if they were changed into blocks of wood,
Unable to move a step, or cry
To the children merrily skipping by,
—Could only follow with the eye
The joyous crowd at the Piper's back.
But how the Mayor was on the rack,
And the wretched Council's bosoms beat,
As the Piper turned from the High Street
To where the Weser rolled its waters
Right in the way of their sons and daughters!
However, he turned from South to West,
And to Koppelberg Hill his steps addressed,
And after him the children pressed;
Great was the joy in every breast.
"He never can cross that mighty top!
He's forced to let the piping drop,
And we shall see our children stop!"
When, lo, as they reached the mountain-side,
A wondrous portal opened wide,
As if a cavern was suddenly hollowed;

And the Piper advanced and the children
       followed,
And when all were in to the very last,
The door in the mountain-side shut fast.
Did I say, all! No! One was lame,
   And could not dance the whole of the way;
And in after years, if you would blame
   His sadness, he was used to say,—
"It's dull in our town since my playmates left!
I can't forget that I'm bereft
Of all the pleasant sights they see,
Which the Piper also promised me.
For he led us, he said, to a joyous land,
Joining the town and just at hand,
Where waters gushed and fruit-trees grew,
And flowers put forth a fairer hue,
And everything was bright and new;
The sparrows were brighter than peacocks
       here,
And their dogs outran our fallow deer,
And honey-bees had lost their stings,
And horses were born with eagles' wings:
And just as I became assured
My lame foot would be speedily cured,
The music stopped and I stood still,
And found myself outside the hill,
Left alone against my will,

To go now limping as before,
And never hear of that country more!"

Alas, alas for Hamelin!
   There came into many a burgher's pate
   A text which says that heaven's gate
   Opes to the rich at as easy rate
As the needle's eye takes a camel in!
The Mayor sent East, West, North and South,
To offer the Piper, by word of mouth,
   Wherever it was men's lot to find him,
Silver and gold to his heart's content,
If he'd only return the way he went,
   And bring the children behind him.
But when they saw 'twas a lost endeavour,
And Piper and dancers were gone for ever,
They made a decree that lawyers never
   Should think their records dated duly
If, after the day of the month and year,
These words did not as well appear,
"And so long after what happened here
   On the Twenty-second of July,
Thirteen hundred and seventy-six:"
And the better in memory to fix
The place of the children's last retreat,

They called it, the Pied Piper's Street—
Where anyone playing on pipe or tabor
Was sure for the future to lose his labour.
Nor suffered they hostelry or tavern
    To shock with mirth a street so solemn;
But opposite the place of the cavern
    They wrote the story on a column,
And on the great church-window painted
The same, to make the world acquainted
How their children were stolen away,
And there it stands to this very day.
And I must not omit to say
That in Transylvania there's a tribe
Of alien people who ascribe
The outlandish ways and dress
On which their neighbours lay such stress,
To their fathers and mothers having risen
Out of some subterraneous prison
In which they were trepanned
Long time ago in a mighty band
Out of Hamelin town in Brunswick land,
But how or why, they don't understand.

x v

So, Willy, let me and you be wipers
Of scores out with all men—especially
        pipers!

And, whether they pipe us free fróm rats or
    fróm mice,
If we've promised them aught, let us keep
    our promise!

— ROBERT BROWNING

Lullaby

Golden slumbers kiss your eyes,
Smiles awake you when you rise.
Sleep, pretty wantons; do not cry,
And I will sing a lullaby:
Rock them, rock them, lullaby.

Care is heavy, therefore sleep you;
You are care, and care must keep you.
Sleep, pretty wantons; do not cry,
And I will sing a lullaby:
Rock them, rock them, lullaby.

— THOMAS DEKKER

FIVE

Faith,
Religion,
and
Meditation

Some Keep the Sabbath Going to Church

Some keep the Sabbath going to Church—
I keep it, staying at Home—
With a Bobolink for a Chorister—
And an Orchard, for a Dome—

Some keep the Sabbath in Surplice—
I just wear my Wings—
And instead of tolling the Bell, for Church,
Our little Sexton—sings.

God preaches, a noted Clergyman—
And the sermon is never long,
So instead of getting to Heaven, at last—
I'm going, all along.

— EMILY DICKINSON

My Heart Leaps Up When I Behold

My heart leaps up when I behold
   A rainbow in the sky;
So was it when my life began;
So is it now I am a man;

So be it when I shall grow old,
   Or let me die!
The Child is father of the Man;
And I could wish my days to be
Bound each to each by natural piety.

— WILLIAM WORDSWORTH

Anthem for Doomed Youth

What passing-bells for these who die as
    cattle?
Only the monstrous anger of the guns.
Only the stuttering rifles' rapid rattle
Can patter out their hasty orisons.
No mockeries now for them; no prayers nor
    bells,
Nor any voice of mourning save the choirs—
The shrill, demented choirs of wailing shells;
And bugles calling for them from sad shires.

What candles may be held to speed them all?
Not in the hands of boys, but in their eyes
Shall shine the holy glimmers of good-byes.

The pallor of girls' brows shall be their pall;
Their flowers the tenderness of patient
      minds,
And each slow dusk a drawing-down of
      blinds.

— WILFRED OWEN

Invictus

Out of the night that covers me,
   Black as the pit from pole to pole,
I thank whatever gods may be
   For my unconquerable soul.

In the fell clutch of circumstance
   I have not winced nor cried aloud.
Under the bludgeonings of chance
   My head is bloody, but unbowed.

Beyond this place of wrath and tears
   Looms but the horror of the shade,
And yet the menace of the years
   Finds and shall find me unafraid.

It matters not how strait the gate,
    How charged with punishment the scroll,
I am the master of my fate:
    I am the captain of my soul.

— WILLIAM ERNEST HENLEY

Remember

Remember me when I am gone away,
    Gone far away into the silent land;
    When you can no more hold me by the
        hand,
Nor I half turn to go yet turning stay.
Remember me when no more day by day
    You tell me of our future that you planned:
    Only remember me; you understand
It will be late to counsel then or pray.
Yet if you should forget me for a while
    And afterwards remember, do not grieve:
    For if the darkness and corruption leave
    A vestige of the thoughts that once I had,

Better by far you should forget and smile
  Than that you should remember and be
    sad.

— Christina Georgina Rossetti

In Flanders Fields

In Flanders fields the poppies blow
Between the crosses, row on row,
  That mark our place; and in the sky
  The larks, still bravely singing, fly
Scarce heard amid the guns below.

We are the Dead. Short days ago
We lived, felt dawn, saw sunset glow,
  Loved and were loved, and now we lie
  In Flanders fields.

Take up our quarrel with the foe:
To you from failing hands we throw
  The torch; be yours to hold it high.

If ye break faith with us who die
We shall not sleep, though poppies grow
In Flanders fields.

— JOHN MCCRAE

The Oxen

Christmas Eve, and twelve of the clock.
   "Now they are all on their knees,"
An elder said as we sat in a flock
   By the embers in hearthside ease.

We pictured the meek mild creatures where
   They dwelt in their strawy pen,
Nor did it occur to one of us there
   To doubt they were kneeling then.

So fair a fancy few would weave
   In these years! Yet, I feel,
If someone said on Christmas Eve,
   "Come; see the oxen kneel

"In the lonely barton by yonder coomb
    Our childhood used to know,"
I should go with him in the gloom,
    Hoping it might be so.

— THOMAS   HARDY

Pied Beauty

Glory be to God for dappled things—
    For skies of couple-colour as a brinded
        cow;
        For rose-moles all in stipple upon trout
            that swim;
Fresh-firecoal chestnut-falls; finches' wings;
    Landscape plotted and pieced—fold, fallow
        and plow;
        And all trades, their gear and tackle and
            trim.

All things counter, original, spare, strange;
    Whatever is fickle, freckled (who knows
        how?)

With swift, slow; sweet, sour; adazzle,
   dim;
He fathers-forth whose beauty is past change:
   Praise him.

— GERARD MANLEY HOPKINS

The Elixir

Teach me, my God and King,
   In all things thee to see,
And what I do in any thing,
   To do it as for thee:

Not rudely as a beast,
   To run into an action;
But still to make thee prepossest,
   And give it his perfection.

A man that looks on glass,
   On it may stay his eye;
Or if he pleaseth, through it pass
   And then the heaven espy.

All may of thee partake:
  Nothing can be so mean,
Which with his tincture (for thy sake)
  Will not grow bright and clean.

A servant with this clause
  Makes drudgery divine:
Who sweeps a room, as for thy laws,
  Makes that and the action fine.

This is the famous stone
  That turneth all to gold:
For that which God doth touch and own
  Cannot for less be told.

— GEORGE HERBERT

Prospice

Fear death?—to feel the fog in my throat,
  The mist in my face,
When the snows begin, and the blasts denote
  I am nearing the place,

The power of the night, the press of the
      storm,
  The post of the foe;
Where he stands, the Arch Fear in a visible
      form,
  Yet the strong man must go:
For the journey is done and the summit
      attained,
  And the barriers fall,
Though a battle's to fight ere the guerdon be
      gained,
  The reward of it all.
I was ever a fighter, so—one fight more,
  The best and the last!
I would hate that death bandaged my eyes,
      and forbore,
  And bade me creep past,
No! let me taste the whole of it, fare like my
      peers
  The heroes of old,
Bear the brunt, in a minute pay glad life's
      arrears
  Of pain, darkness and cold.
For sudden the worst turns the best to the
      brave,
  The black minute's at end,

And the elements' rage, the fiend-voices that
      rave,
   Shall dwindle, shall blend,
Shall change, shall become first a peace out of
      pain,
   Then a light, then thy breast,
O thou soul of my soul! I shall clasp thee
      again,
   And with God be the rest!

— Robert Browning

Redemption

Having been tenant long to a rich Lord,
   Not thriving, I resolved to be bold,
   And make a suit unto him, to afford
A new small-rented lease and cancel the old.
In heaven at his manor I him sought:
   They told me there that he was lately gone
   About some land, which he had dearly
      bought
Long since on earth, to take possession.

I straight returned, and knowing his great
    birth,
  Sought him accordingly in great resorts;
  In cities, theaters, gardens, parks, and
    courts:
At length I heard a ragged noise and mirth
  Of thieves and murderers; there I him
    espied,
  Who straight, "Your suit is granted," said,
    and died.

— GEORGE HERBERT

After Great Pain, a Formal Feeling Comes

After great pain, a formal feeling comes—
The Nerves sit ceremonious, like Tombs—
The stiff Heart questions was it He, that bore,
And Yesterday, or Centuries before?

The Feet, mechanical, go round—
Of Ground, or Air, or Ought—
A Wooden way

Regardless grown,
A Quartz contentment, like a stone—

This is the Hour of Lead—
Remembered, if outlived,
As Freezing persons, recollect the Snow—
First—Chill—then Stupor—then the letting
    go—

— EMILY DICKINSON

The Road Not Taken

Two roads diverged in a yellow wood,
And sorry I could not travel both
And be one traveler, long I stood
And looked down one as far as I could
To where it bent in the undergrowth;

Then took the other, as just as fair,
And having perhaps the better claim,
Because it was grassy and wanted wear;
Though as for that the passing there
Had worn them really about the same,

And both that morning equally lay
In leaves no step had trodden black.
Oh, I kept the first for another day!
Yet knowing how way leads on to way,
I doubted if I should ever come back.

I shall be telling this with a sigh
Somewhere ages and ages hence:
Two roads diverged in a wood, and I—
I took the one less traveled by,
And that has made all the difference.

— ROBERT FROST

The Anvil—God's Word

Last eve I passed beside a blacksmith's door,
   And heard the anvil ring the vesper chime;
Then, looking in, I saw upon the floor
   Old hammers, worn with beating years of
    time.

"How many anvils have you had," said I,
   "To wear and batter all these hammers so?"

"Just one," said he, and then, with twinkling
    eye,
  "The anvil wears the hammers out, you
    know."

And so, thought I, the anvil of God's Word,
  For ages skeptic blows have beat upon;
Yet, though the noise of falling blows was
    heard,
The anvil is unharmed—the hammers gone.

— ANONYMOUS

The Lamb

  Little Lamb, who made thee?
  Dost thou know who made thee?
Gave thee life, and bid thee feed
By the stream and o'er the mead;
Gave thee clothing of delight,
Softest clothing, woolly, bright;
Gave thee such a tender voice,
Making all the vales rejoice?
  Little Lamb, who made thee?
  Dost thou know who made thee?

Little Lamb, I'll tell thee,
Little Lamb, I'll tell thee:
He is callèd by thy name,
For he calls himself a Lamb,
He is meek, and he is mild;
He became a little child.
I a child, and thou a lamb.
We are callèd by his name.
　Little Lamb, God bless thee!
　Little Lamb, God bless thee!

— WILLIAM BLAKE

When I Have Fears That I May Cease to Be

When I have fears that I may cease to be
　Before my pen has gleaned my teeming
　　brain,
Before high-pilèd books, in charactry,
　Hold like rich garners the full ripen'd grain;
When I behold, upon the night's starr'd face,
　Huge cloudy symbols of a high romance,

And think that I may never live to trace
   Their shadows, with the magic hand of
      chance;
And when I feel, fair creature of an hour!
   That I shall never look upon thee more,
Never have relish in the faery power
   Of unreflecting love;—then on the shore
Of the wide world I stand alone, and think
Till Love and Fame to nothingness do sink.

— JOHN KEATS

If—

If you can keep your head when all about you
   Are losing theirs and blaming it on you;
If you can trust yourself when all men doubt
      you,
   But make allowance for their doubting too;
If you can wait and not be tired by waiting,
   Or, being lied about, don't deal in lies,
Or, being hated, don't give way to hating,
   And yet don't look too good, nor talk too
      wise;

• • •

If you can dream—and not make dreams
    your master;
  If you can think—and not make thoughts
    your aim;
If you can meet with triumph and disaster
  And treat those two impostors just the
    same;
If you can bear to hear the truth you've
    spoken
  Twisted by knaves to make a trap for fools,
Or watch the things you gave your life to
    broken,
  And stoop and build 'em up with wornout
    tools;

If you can make one heap of all your
    winnings
  And risk it on one turn of pitch-and-toss,
And lose, and start again at your beginnings
  And never breathe a word about your loss;
If you can force your heart and nerve and
    sinew
  To serve your turn long after they are gone,
And so hold on when there is nothing in you
  Except the Will which says to them: "Hold
    on";

If you can talk with crowds and keep your
     virtue,
  Or walk with kings—nor lose the common
     touch;
If neither foes nor loving friends can hurt
     you;
  If all men count with you, but none too
     much;
If you can fill the unforgiving minute
  With sixty seconds' worth of distance run—
Yours is the Earth and everything that's in it,
  And—which is more—you'll be a Man, my
     son!

— RUDYARD KIPLING

A Man Saw a Ball of Gold

A man saw a ball of gold in the sky;
He climbed for it,
And eventually he achieved it—
It was clay.

• • •

Now this is the strange part:
When the man went to the earth
And looked again,
Lo, there was the ball of gold.
Now this is the strange part:
It was a ball of gold.
Ay, by the heavens, it was a ball of gold.

— STEPHEN CRANE

Ode on Solitude

Happy the man, whose wish and care
    A few paternal acres bound,
Content to breathe his native air,
        In his own ground.

Whose herds with milk, whose fields with
        bread,
    Whose flocks supply him with attire,
Whose trees in summer yield him shade,
        In winter fire.

Blest, who can unconcern'dly find
    Hours, days, and years slide soft away,

In health of body, peace of mind,
        Quiet by day,

Sound sleep by night; study and ease,
   Together mixt; sweet recreation;
And innocence, which most does please
        With meditation.

Thus let me live, unseen, unknown;
   Thus unlamented let me die;
Steal from the world, and not a stone
        Tell where I lie.

      — ALEXANDER POPE

Up-Hill

Does the road wind up-hill all the way?
   Yes, to the very end.
Will the day's journey take the whole long
     day?
From morn to night, my friend.

But is there for the night a resting-place?
   A roof for when the slow dark hours begin.

May not the darkness hide it from my face?
You cannot miss that inn.

Shall I meet other wayfarers at night?
Those who have gone before.
Then must I knock, or call when just in sight?
They will not keep you standing at that
*   door.*

Shall I find comfort, travel-sore and weak?
Of labour you shall find the sum.
Will there be beds for me and all who seek?
Yea, beds for all who come.

— CHRISTINA GEORGINA ROSSETTI

Dream Deferred

What happens to a dream deferred?

Does it dry up
like a raisin in the sun?
Or fester like a sore—
And then run?

Does it stink like rotten meat?
Or crust and sugar over—
like a syrupy sweet?

Maybe it just sags
like a heavy load.

Or does it explode?

— LANGSTON HUGHES

Rock of Ages

Rock of Ages, cleft for me,
Let me hide myself in Thee!
Let the water and the blood,
From Thy riven side which flow'd,
Be of sin the double cure,
Cleanse me from its guilt and power.

Not the labors of my hands
Can fulfil Thy law's demands;
Could my zeal no respite know,
Could my tears for ever flow,

All for sin could not atone;
Thou must save, and Thou alone.

Nothing in my hand I bring;
Simply to Thy Cross I cling;
Naked, come to Thee for dress;
Helpless, look to Thee for grace;
Foul, I to the Fountain fly;
Wash me, Saviour, or I die!

While I draw this fleeting breath,
When my eyestrings break in death,
When I soar through tracts unknown,
See Thee on Thy judgment-throne;
Rock of Ages, cleft for me,
Let me hide myself in Thee!

— AUGUSTUS MONTAGUE TOPLADY

"I Have a Rendezvous with Death"

I have a rendezvous with Death
At some disputed barricade,
When Spring comes back with rustling shade

And apple-blossoms fill the air—
I have a rendezvous with Death
When Spring brings back blue days and fair.

It may be he shall take my hand
And lead me into his dark land
And close my eyes and quench my breath—
It may be I shall pass him still.
I have a rendezvous with Death
On some scarred slope of battered hill,
When Spring comes round again this year
And the first meadow-flowers appear.

God knows 'twere better to be deep
Pillowed in silk and scented down,
Where Love throbs out in blissful sleep,
Pulse nigh to pulse, and breath to breath,
Where hushed awakenings are dear . . .
But I've a rendezvous with Death
At midnight in some flaming town,
When Spring trips north again this year,
And I to my pledged word am true,
I shall not fail that rendezvous.

— ALAN SEEGER

Divina Commedia

Oft have I seen at some cathedral door
   A laborer, pausing in the dust and heat,
   Lay down his burden, and with reverent
      feet
Enter, and cross himself, and on the floor
Kneel to repeat his paternoster o'er;
   Far off the noises of the world retreat;
   The loud vociferations of the street
Become an undistinguishable roar.
So, as I enter here from day to day,
   And leave my burden at this minster gate,
Kneeling in prayer, and not ashamed to pray,
   The tumult of the time disconsolate
To inarticulate murmurs dies away,
   While the eternal ages watch and wait.

— HENRY WADSWORTH
LONGFELLOW

When I Heard the Learn'd Astronomer

When I heard the learn'd astronomer,
When the proofs, the figures, were ranged in
    columns before me,
When I was shown the charts and diagrams,
    to add, divide, and measure them,
When I sitting heard the astronomer where
    he lectured with much applause in the
    lecture-room,
How soon unaccountable I became tired and
    sick,
Till rising and gliding out I wander'd off by
    myself,
In the mystical moist night-air, and from time
    to time,
Look'd up in perfect silence at the stars.

— WALT WHITMAN

Death Be Not Proud

Death be not proud, though some have
    called thee
Mighty and dreadful, for thou art not so,

For those, whom thou thinkest thou dost
      overthrow,
Die not, poor death, nor yet canst thou kill
      me.
From rest and sleep, which but thy pictures
      be,
Much pleasure, then from thee much more
      must flow,
And soonest our best men with thee do go,
Rest of their bones and soul's delivery.
Thou art slave to Fate, chance, kings and
      desperate men,
And dost with poison, war, and sickness
      dwell,
And poppy or charms can make us sleep as
      well
And better than thy stroke; why swellest thou
      then?
One short sleep past, we wake eternally,
And death shall be no more; Death thou shalt
      die.

— JOHN DONNE

I May, I Might, I Must

If you will tell me why the fen
appears impassable, I then
will tell you why I think that I
can get across it if I try.

— MARIANNE MOORE

On His Seventy-fifth Birthday

I strove with none; for none was worth my
    strife.
Nature I loved, and next to Nature, Art;
I warmed both hands before the fire of life,
It sinks, and I am ready to depart.

— WALTER SAVAGE LANDOR

Happy Thought

The world is so full of a number of things,
I'm sure we should all be as happy as kings.

— ROBERT LOUIS STEVENSON

Requiem

Under the wide and starry sky
Dig the grave and let me lie.
Glad did I live and gladly die,
   And I laid me down with a will.

This be the verse you grave for me:
Here he lies where he longed to be;
Home is the sailor, home from sea,
   And the hunter home from the hill.

— ROBERT LOUIS STEVENSON

My Triumph

Sweeter than any sung
My songs that found no tongue;
Nobler than any fact
My wish that failed to act.

Others shall sing the song,
Other shall right the wrong,—
Finish what I begin,
And all I fail of win.

— JOHN GREENLEAF WHITTIER

Sometimes I Feel Like a Motherless Child

Sometimes I feel like a motherless child,
Sometimes I feel like a motherless child,
Sometimes I feel like a motherless child,
A long ways from home,
A long way from home.
True believer,
A long ways from home.
A long way from home.

Sometimes I feel like I'm almost gone,
Sometimes I feel like I'm almost gone,
Sometimes I feel like I'm almost gone,
Way up in the heavenly land,
Way up in the heavenly land.
True believer,
Way up in the heavenly land,
Way up in the heavenly land.

Sometimes I feel like a motherless child,
Sometimes I feel like a motherless child,
Sometimes I feel like a motherless child,
A long ways from home,
A long way from home.
True believer,
A long ways from home.
A long way from home.

— Anonymous

Wit, Humor,
and
Just Plain
Verbal Fun

The Moron

See the happy moron,
He doesn't give a damn!
I wish I were a moron—
My God! Perhaps I am!

— ANONYMOUS

Get Up, Get Up

Get up, get up, you lazy-head,
  Get up you lazy sinner,
We need those sheets for tablecloths,
  It's nearly time for dinner.

— ANONYMOUS

Marriage Couplet

I think of my wife, and I think of Lot,
And I think of the lucky break he got.

— WILLIAM COLE

Too Great a Sacrifice

The maid, as by the papers doth appear,
Whom fifty thousand dollars made so dear,
To test Lothario's passion, simply said,
"Forego the weed before we go to wed.
For smoke, take flame; I'll be that flame's
        bright fanner.
To have your Anna, give up your Havana."
But he, when thus she brought him to the
        scratch,
Lit his cigar, and threw away his match.

— Anonymous

To a Segar

Sweet antidote to sorrow, toil and strife,
Charm against discontent and wrinkled care,
Who knows thy power can never know
        despair;
Who knows thee not, one solace lacks of life:
When cares oppress, or when the busy day
Gives place to tranquil eve, a single puff
Can drive ev'n want and lassitude away,

And give a mourner happiness enough.
From thee when curling clouds of incense
      rise,
They hide each evil that in prospect lies;
But when in evanescence fades thy smoke,
Ah! what, dear sedative, my cares shall
      smother?
If thou evaporate, the charm is broke,
Till I, departing taper, light another.

— SAMUEL LOW

Dried-Apple Pies

I loathe, abhor, detest, despise,
Abominate dried-apple pies.
I like good bread, I like good meat,
Or anything that's fit to eat;
But of all poor grub beneath the skies,
The poorest is dried-apple pies.
Give me the toothache, or sore eyes,
But don't give me dried-apple pies.
The farmer takes his gnarliest fruit,
'Tis wormy, bitter, and hard, to boot;
He leaves the hulls to make us cough,

And don't take half the peeling off.
Then on a dirty cord 'tis strung
And in a garret window hung,
And there it serves as roost for flies,
Until it's made up into pies.
Tread on my corns, or tell me lies,
But don't pass me dried-apple pies.

— ANONYMOUS

Disgusting

At the boarding house where I live
Things are getting very old.
Long gray hairs in the butter,
And the cheese is green with mold,
When the dog died we had sausage,
When the cat died, catnip tea.
When the landlord died I left it;
Spareribs are too much for me.

— ANONYMOUS

Three Young Rats with Black Felt Hats

Three young rats with black felt hats,
Three young ducks with white straw flats,
Three young dogs with curling tails,
Three young cats with demi-veils
Went out to walk with two young pigs
In satin vests and sorrel wings,
But suddenly it chanced to rain
And so they all went home again.

— ANONYMOUS

There Was a Man So Wise

There was a Man so wise,
He jumpt into
A Bramble Bush,
And scratcht out both his eyes.
And when he saw,
His Eyes were out,
And had reason to Complain,
He jumpt into a Quickset Hedge,
And Scratcht them in again.

— ANONYMOUS

The Pobble Who Has No Toes

The Pobble who has no toes
  Had once as many as we;
When they said, "Some day you may lose
     them all";—
    He replied,—"Fish fiddle de-dee!"
And his Aunt Jobiska made him drink,
Lavender water tinged with pink,
For she said, "The World in general knows
There's nothing so good for a Pobble's toes!"

The Pobble who has no toes,
  Swam across the Bristol Channel;
But before he set out he wrapped his nose
  In a piece of scarlet flannel.
For his Aunt Jobiska said, "No harm
Can come to his toes if his nose is warm;
And it's perfectly known that a Pobble's toes
Are safe,—provided he minds his nose."

The Pobble swam fast and well
    And when boats or ships came near him
He tinkledy-binkledy-winkled a bell
  So that all the world could hear him.
And all the Sailors and Admirals cried,

When they saw him nearing the further
        side,—
"He has gone to fish, for his Aunt Jobiska's
Runcible Cat with crimson whiskers!"

But before he touched the shore,
    The shore of Bristol Channel,
A sea-green Porpoise carried away
    His wrapper of scarlet flannel.
And when he came to observe his feet
Formerly garnished with toes so neat
His face at once became forlorn
On perceiving that all his toes were gone!

And nobody ever knew
    From that dark day to the present,
Whoso had taken the Pobble's toes,
    In a manner so far from pleasant.
Whether the shrimps or crawfish gray,
Or crafty Mermaids stole them away—
Nobody knew; and nobody knows
How the Pobble was robbed of his twice five
        toes!

The Pobble who has no toes
    Was placed in a friendly Bark,

And they rowed him back, and carried him
    up,
  To his Aunt Jobiska's Park.
And she made him a feast at his earnest wish
Of eggs and buttercups fried with fish;—
And she said,—"It's a fact the whole world
    knows,
That Pobbles are happier without their toes."

— EDWARD LEAR

How Doth the Little Crocodile

How doth the little crocodile
  Improve his shining tail;
And pour the waters of the Nile
  On every golden scale!

How cheerfully he seems to grin,
  How neatly spreads his claws,
And welcomes little fishes in,
  With gently smiling jaws!

— LEWIS CARROLL

The Smoking World

Tobacco is a dirty weed:
   I like it.
It satisfies no normal need:
   I like it.
It makes you thin, it makes you lean,
It takes the hair right off your bean,
It's the worst darn stuff I've ever seen:
   I like it.

— GRAHAM LEE HEMMINGER

Nightmare

When you're lying awake with a dismal
      headache, and repose is taboo'd by
      anxiety,
I conceive you may use any language you
      choose to indulge in, without
      impropriety;
For your brain is on fire—the bedclothes
      conspire of usual slumber to plunder
      you:

First your counterpane goes, and uncovers
      your toes, and your sheet slips
      demurely from under you;
Then the blanketing tickles—you feel like
      mixed pickles—so terribly sharp is the
      pricking,
And you're hot, and you're cross, and you
      tumble and toss till there's nothing
      'twixt you and the ticking.
Then the bedclothes all creep to the ground
      in a heap, and you pick 'em all up in a
      tangle;
Next your pillow resigns and politely
      declines to remain at its usual
      angle!
Well, you get some repose in the form of a
      doze, with hot eyeballs and head ever
      aching,
But your slumbering teems with such
      horrible dreams that you'd very much
      better be waking;
For you dream you are crossing the Channel,
      and tossing about in a steamer from
      Harwich—
Which is something between a large bathing
      machine and a very small second-class
      carriage—

And you're giving a treat (penny ice and cold
      meat) to a party of friends and
      relations—
They're a ravenous horde—and they all came
      on board at Sloane Square and South
      Kensington Stations.
And bound on that journey you find your
      attorney (who started that morning
      from Devon);
He's a bit undersized, and you don't feel
      surprised when he tells you he's only
      eleven.
Well, you're driving like mad with this
      singular lad (by-the-bye the ship's now
      a four-wheeler),
And you're playing round games, and he calls
      you bad names when you tell him that
      'ties pay the dealer';
But this you can't stand, so you throw up your
      hand, and you find you're as cold as an
      icicle,
In your shirt and your socks (the black silk
      with gold clocks), crossing Salisbury
      Plain on a bicycle:
And he and the crew are on bicycles too—
      which they've somehow or other
      invested in—

And he's telling the tars, all the particu*lars* of
a company he's interested in—
It's a scheme of devices, to get at low prices,
all goods from cough mixtures to cables
(Which tickled the sailors) by treating
retailers, as though they were all
vege*t*ables—
You get a good spadesman to plant a small
tradesman, (first take off his boots with
a boot-tree),
And his legs will take root, and his fingers
will shoot, and they'll blossom and bud
like a fruit-tree—
From the greengrocer tree you get grapes and
green pea, cauliflower, pineapple, and
cranberries,
While the pastrycook plant, cherry brandy
will grant, apple puffs, and three-
corners, and banberries—
The shares are a penny, and ever so many are
taken by Rothschild and Baring,
And just as a few are allotted to you, you
awake with a shudder despairing—
You're a regular wreck, with a crick in your
neck, and no wonder you snore, for
your head's on the floor, and you've
needles and pins from your soles to

your shins, and your flesh is a-creep for
your left leg's asleep, and you've cramp
in your toes, and a fly on your nose,
and some fluff in your lung, and a
feverish tongue, and a thirst that's
intense, and a general sense that you
haven't been sleeping in clover;
But the darkness has passed, and it's daylight
at last, and the night has been long—
ditto ditto my song—and thank
goodness they're both of them over!

— W. S. GILBERT

Horse Sense

A horse can't pull while kicking.
    This fact I merely mention.
And he can't kick while pulling,
    Which is my chief contention.

Let's imitate the good old horse
    And lead a life that's fitting;
Just pull an honest load, and then
    There'll be no time for kicking.

— ANONYMOUS

Limericks

His sister, called Lucy O'Finner,
Grew constantly thinner and thinner;
  The reason was plain,
  She slept out in the rain,
And was never allowed any dinner.

— Lewis Carroll

*   *   *

I'd rather have fingers than toes,
I'd rather have ears than a nose;
  As for my hair,
  I'm glad it's still there,
I'll be awfully sad when it goes.

— Gelett Burgess

*   *   *

There was a young lady of Ryde,
Who ate some green apples and died;
  The apples fermented
  Inside the lamented,
And made cider inside her inside.

— Anonymous

A man hired by John Smith and Co.
Loudly declared that he'd tho.
    Men that he saw
    Dumping dirt near his door—
The drivers, therefore, didn't do.

— MARK TWAIN

*   *   *

There was an old man of Tarentum,
Who gnashed his false teeth till he bent 'em:
    And when asked for the cost
    Of what he had lost,
Said, "I really can't tell, for I rent 'em!"

There were three young women of
        Birmingham,
And I know a sad story concerning 'em:
    They stuck needles and pins
    In the reverend shins
Of the Bishop engaged in confirming 'em.

    There was a young lady of Wilts,
    Who walked up to Scotland on stilts;

When they said it was shocking
To show so much stocking,
She answered: "Then what about kilts?"

There was a young girl of Lahore,
The same shape behind as before.
  As you never knew where
  To offer a chair,
She had to sit down on the floor.

— COSMO MONKHOUSE

The Common Cormorant

The common cormorant or shag
Lays eggs inside a paper bag
The reason you will see no doubt
It is to keep the lightning out.
But what these unobservant birds
Have never noticed is that herds
Of wandering bears may come with buns
And steal the bags to hold the crumbs.

— ANONYMOUS

My Own Epitaph

Life is a jest, and all things show it;
I thought so once, but now I know it.

— JOHN GAY

The Boy

Down through the snow-drifts in the street
  With blustering joy he steers;
His rubber boots are full of feet
  And his tippet full of ears.

— EUGENE FIELD

Judged by the Company One Keeps

One night in late October,
When I was far from sober,
Returning with my load with manly pride,
My feet began to stutter,
So I lay down in the gutter,
And a pig came near and lay down by my
    side;
A lady passing by was heard to say:
"You can tell a man who boozes,
By the company he chooses,"
And the pig got up and slowly walked away.

— ANONYMOUS

The Height of the Ridiculous

I wrote some lines once on a time
   In a wondrous merry mood,
And thought, as usual, men would say
   They were exceeding good.

They were so queer, so very queer,
   I laughed as I would die;

Albeit, in the general way,
  A sober man am I.

I called my servant, and he came;
  How kind it was of him,
To mind a slender man like me,
  He of the mighty limb!

"These to the printer," I exclaimed,
  And, in my humorous way,
I added (as a trifling jest),
  "There'll be the devil to pay."

He took the paper, and I watched,
  And saw him peep within;
At the first line he read, his face
  Was all upon a grin.

He read the next, the grin grew broad,
  And shot from ear to ear;
He read the third, a chuckling noise
  I now began to hear.

The fourth, he broke into a roar;
  The fifth, his waistband split;
The sixth, he burst five buttons off,
  And tumbled in a fit.

Ten days and nights, with sleepless eye,
   I watched that wretched man,
And since, I never dare to write
   As funny as I can.

— OLIVER WENDELL HOLMES

The Owl and the Pussy-Cat

The Owl and the Pussy-cat went to sea
   In a beautiful pea-green boat,
They took some honey, and plenty of money
   Wrapped up in a five-pound note.
The Owl looked up to the stars above,
   And sang to a small guitar,
"O lovely Pussy! O Pussy, my love,
   What a beautiful Pussy you are,
     You are,
     You are!
   What a beautiful Pussy you are!"

Pussy said to the Owl, "You elegant fowl!
   How charmingly sweet you sing!
O let us be married! too long we have tarried:
   But what shall we do for a ring?"

They sailed away, for a year and a day,
    To the land where the Bong-tree grows
And there in a wood a Piggy-wig stood
    With a ring at the end of his nose,
        His nose,
        His nose,
    With a ring at the end of his nose.

"Dear Pig, are you willing to sell for one
        shilling
    Your ring?" Said the Piggy, "I will."
So they took it away, and were married next
        day
    By the Turkey who lives on the hill.
They dined on mince, and slices of quince,
    Which they ate with a runcible spoon;
And hand in hand, on the edge of the sand,
    They danced by the light of the moon,
        The moon,
        The moon,
    They danced by the light of the moon.

— EDWARD LEAR

The Bells

Hear the sledges with the bells—
   Silver bells!
What a world of merriment their melody
    foretells!

How they tinkle, tinkle, tinkle,
   In the icy air of night!
While the stars that oversprinkle
All the heavens seem to twinkle
   With a crystalline delight;
   Keeping time, time, time,
   In a sort of Runic rhyme,
To the tintinnabulation that so musically
    wells
From the bells, bells, bells, bells
   Bells, bells, bells—
From the jingling and the tinkling of the
    bells.

Hear the mellow wedding bells—
  Golden bells!
What a world of happiness their harmony
  foretells!
 Through the balmy air of night
 How they ring out their delight!—
 From the molten-golden notes,
  And all in tune,
 What a liquid ditty floats
To the turtle-dove that listens, while she
  gloats
  On the moon!
Oh, from out the sounding cells,
What a gush of euphony voluminously wells!
 How it swells!
 How it dwells
On the Future!—how it tells
Of the rapture that impels
To the swinging and the ringing
Of the bells, bells, bells—
Of the bells, bells, bells, bells,
 Bells, bells, bells—
To the rhyming and the chiming of the bells!

Hear the loud alarum bells—
  Brazen bells!
What a tale of terror, now their turbulency
    tells
In the startled ear of night
How they scream out their affright!
  Too much horrified to speak,
  They can only shriek, shriek,
  Out of tune,
In a clamorous appealing to the mercy of the
    fire,
In a mad expostulation with the deaf and
    frantic fire,
Leaping higher, higher, higher,
With a desperate desire,
And a resolute endeavour
Now—now to sit, or never,
By the side of the pale-faced moon.
Oh, the bells, bells, bells!
What a tale their terror tells
  Of Despair!
How they clang, and clash, and roar!
What a horror they outpour
On the bosom of the palpitating air!

Yet the ear, it fully knows,
  By the twanging,
  And the clanging,
How the danger ebbs and flows;
Yet the ear distinctly tells,
  In the jangling,
  And the wrangling,
How the danger sinks and swells,
By the sinking or the swelling in the anger of
      the bells—
  Of the bells—
Of the bells, bells, bells, bells,
  Bells, bells, bells—
In the clamor and the clanging of the bells!

                    I V

Hear the tolling of the bells—
  Iron bells!
What a world of solemn thought their monody
      compels!
In the silence of the night,
How we shiver with affright
At the melancholy menace of their tone!
For every sound that floats
From the rust within their throats
  Is a groan.

And the people—ah, the people—
They that dwell up in the steeple,
    All alone.
And who tolling, tolling, tolling,
    In that muffled monotone,
Feel a glory in so rolling
    On the human heart a stone—
They are neither man nor woman—
They are neither brute nor human—
    They are Ghouls:—
And their king is who tolls;—
And he rolls, rolls, rolls,
    Rolls
A paean from the bells!
And his merry bosom swells
With the paean of the bells!
And he dances, and he yells;
    Keeping time, time, time,
    In a sort of Runic rhyme,
To the paean of the bells:—
    Of the bells:
Keeping time, time, time,
In a sort of Runic rhyme,
To the throbbing of the bells—
Of the bells, bells, bells—
To the sobbing of the bells:—
Keeping time, time, time,

As he knells, knells, knells,
In a happy Runic rhyme,
To the rolling of the bells—
Of the bells, bells, bells:—
To the tolling of the bells—
Of the bells, bells, bells, bells,
    Bells, bells, bells—
To the moaning and the groaning of the bells.

— EDGAR ALLAN POE

·SEVEN·

Americana

The Hasty Pudding

Let the green Succotash with thee contend,
Let beans and corn their sweetest juices
     blend,
Let butter drench them in its yellow tide,
And a long slice of bacon grace their side;
Not all the plate, how fam'd soe'er it be,
Can please my palate like a bowl of thee.

Some talk of Hoe-cake, fair Virginia's pride,
Rich Johnny-cake this mouth has often tried;
Both please me well, their virtues much the
     same;
Alike their fabric, as allied their fame,
Except in dear New-England, where the last
Receives a dash of pumpkin in the paste,
To give it sweetness and improve the taste.
But place them all before me, smoking hot,
The big round dumpling rolling from the pot;
The pudding of the bag, whose quivering
     breast,
With suet lined leads on the Yankee feast;
The Charlotte brown, within whose crusty
     sides

A belly soft the pulpy apple hides;
The yellow bread, whose face like amber
    glows,
And all of Indian that the bake-pan knows—
You tempt me not—my fav'rite greets my
    eyes,
To that loved bowl my spoon by instinct flies.

— JOEL BARLOW

Yankee Doodle

Yankee Doodle went to town
    Riding on a pony,
Stuck a feather in his cap
    And called it "macaroni."

CHORUS:

Yankee Doodle, keep it up,
Yankee Doodle, dandy,
Mind the music and the step,
And with the girls be handy.

232

Father and I went down to camp,
  Along with Captain Gooding,
And there we see the men and boys,
  As thick as hasty pudding.

And there we see a thousand men,
  As rich as 'Squire David;
And what they wasted every day,
  I wish it could be saved.

The 'lasses they eat every day.
  Would keep a house in winter,
They have so much that, I'll be bound,
  They eat it when they're a mind to.

And there we see a swamping gun,
  Large as a log of maple,
Upon a deuced little cart,
  A load for father's cattle.

And every time they shot it off,
  It takes a horn of powder,
And makes a noise like father's gun,
  Only a nation louder.

— ANONYMOUS

America

My country, 'tis of thee,
Sweet land of liberty,
    Of thee I sing;
Land where my fathers died,
Land of the pilgrims' pride,
From every mountain-side
    Let freedom ring.

My native country, thee,
Land of the noble free,
    Thy name I love;
I love thy rocks and rills,
Thy woods and templed hills;
My heart with rapture thrills,
    Like that above.

Let music swell the breeze,
And ring from all the trees
    Sweet freedom's song;
Let mortal tongues awake,
Let all that breathe partake,
Let rocks their silence break.—
    The sound prolong.

Our fathers' God, to Thee,
Author of liberty,
　　To Thee we sing;
Long may our land be bright
With freedom's holy light;
Protect us by Thy might,
　　Great God, our King.

— SAMUEL FRANCIS SMITH

America the Beautiful

O beautiful for spacious skies,
　　For amber waves of grain,
For purple mountain majesties
　　Above the fruited plain!
America! America!
　　God shed His grace on thee
And crown thy good with brotherhood
　　From sea to shining sea!

O beautiful for pilgrim feet,
　　Whose stern, impassioned stress

A thoroughfare for freedom beat
  Across the wilderness!
America! America!
  God mend thine every flaw,
Confirm thy soul in self-control,
  Thy liberty in law!

O beautiful for heroes proved
  In liberating strife,
Who more than self their country loved,
  And mercy more than life!
America! America!
  May God thy gold refine,
Till all success be nobleness
  And every gain divine!

O beautiful for patriot dream
  That sees beyond the years
Thine alabaster cities gleam
  Undimmed by human tears!
America! America!
  God shed His grace on thee,
And crown thy good with brotherhood
  From sea to shining sea!

— KATHARINE LEE BATES

The Star-Spangled Banner

Oh, say, can you see, by the dawn's early
    light,
  What so proudly we hailed at the twilight's
    last gleaming,
Whose broad stripes and bright stars through
    the perilous fight,
  O'er the ramparts we watched were so
    gallantly streaming?
And the rockets' red glare, the bombs
    bursting in air,
Gave proof thro' the night that our flag was
    still there.
Oh, say, does that star-spangled banner yet
    wave
O'er the land of the free, and the home of the
    brave!

On the shore, dimly seen thro' the mists of
    the deep,
  Where the foe's haughty host in dread
    silence reposes,
What is that which the breeze o'er the
    towering steep,

As it fitfully blows, half conceals, half
  discloses?
Now it catches the gleam of the morning's
  first beam,
In full glory reflected, now shines on the
  stream.
'Tis the star-spangled banner; oh, long may it
  wave
O'er the land of the free, and the home of the
  brave!

And where is that band who so vauntingly
  swore
  That the havoc of war and the battle's
    confusion
A home and a country should leave us no
  more?
  Their blood has washed out their foul
    footsteps' pollution.
No refuge could save the hireling and slave
From the terror of flight, or the gloom of the
  grave:
And the star-spangled banner in triumph doth
  wave
O'er the land of the free, and the home of the
  brave!

Oh, thus be it ever when freemen shall stand
    Between their loved homes and the war's
        desolation;
Blest with victory and peace, may the
        heaven-rescued land
    Praise the power that hath made and
        preserved us a nation!
Then conquer we must, when our cause it is
        just,
And this be our motto: "In God is our trust!"
And the star-spangled banner in triumph doth
        wave,
O'er the land of the free, and the home of the
        brave!

— FRANCIS SCOTT KEY

Tribute to America

There is a people mighty in its youth,
    A land beyond the oceans of the west,
Where, though with rudest rites, Freedom
        and Truth

Are Worshipt. From a glorious mother's
    breast,
  Who, since high Athens fell, among the rest
Sate like the Queen of Nations, but in woe,
  By inbred monsters outraged and opprest,
Turns to her chainless child for succor now,
It draws the milk of power in Wisdom's
    fullest flow.

That land is like an eagle, whose young gaze
  Feeds on the noontide beam, whose golden
    plume
Floats moveless on the storm, and on the
    blaze
  Of sunrise gleams when Earth is wrapt in
    gloom;
  An epitaph of glory for thy tomb
Of murdered Europe may thy fame be made,
Great People! As the sands shalt thou
    become,
Thy growth is swift as morn when night must
    fade;
The multitudinous Earth shall sleep beneath
    thy shade.

Yes, in the desert, there is built a home
  For Freedom! Genius is made strong to
    rear

The monuments of man beneath the dome
  Of a new Heaven; myriads assemble there
  Whom the proud lords of man, in rage or
    fear,
Drive from their wasted homes. The boon I
    pray
  Is this—that Cythna shall be convoyed
    there,—
Nay, start not at the name—America!

— PERCY BYSSHE SHELLEY

Concord Hymn

[SUNG AT THE COMPLETION OF
THE CONCORD MONUMENT,
APRIL 19, 1836]

By the rude bridge that arched the flood,
  Their flag to April's breeze unfurled,
Here once the embattled farmers stood,
  And fired the shot heard round the world.

The foe long since in silence slept;
  Alike the conqueror silent sleeps;

And Time the ruined bridge has swept
  Down the dark stream which seaward
    creeps.

On this green bank, by this soft stream,
  We set to-day a votive stone;
That memory may their deed redeem,
  When, like our sires, our sons are gone.

Spirit, that made those heroes dare
  To die, and leave their children free,
Bid Time and Nature gently spare
  The shaft we raise to them and thee.

— RALPH WALDO EMERSON

Paul Revere's Ride

Listen, my children, and you shall hear
Of the midnight ride of Paul Revere,
On the eighteenth of April, in Seventy-five;
Hardly a man is now alive
Who remembers that famous day and year.

He said to his friend, "If the British march
By land or sea from the town tonight,
Hang a lantern aloft in the belfry arch
Of the North Church tower as a signal light,—
One, if by land, and two, if by sea;
And I on the opposite shore will be,
Ready to ride and spread the alarm
Through every Middlesex village and farm,
For the country folk to be up and to arm."

Then he said, "Good night!" and with
        muffled oar
Silently rowed to the Charlestown shore,
Just as the moon rose over the bay,
Where swinging wide at her moorings lay
The *Somerset,* British man-of-war;
A phantom ship, with each mast and spar
Across the moon like a prison bar,
And a huge black hulk, that was magnified
By its own reflection in the tide.

Meanwhile, his friend through alley and
        street
Wanders and watches, with eager ears,
Till in the silence around him he hears
The muster of men at the barrack door,

The sound of arms, and the tramp of feet,
And the measured tread of the grenadiers,
Marching down to their boats on the shore.

Then he climbed the tower of the Old North
    Church,
By the wooden stairs, with stealthy tread,
To the belfry-chamber overhead,
And startled the pigeons from their perch
On the sombre rafters, that round him made
Masses and moving shapes of shade,—
By the trembling ladder, steep and tall,
To the highest window in the wall,
Where he paused to listen and look down
A moment on the roofs of the town
And the moonlight flowing over all.

Beneath, in the churchyard, lay the dead,
In their night-encampment on the hill,
Wrapped in silence so deep and still
That he could hear, like a sentinel's tread,
The watchful night-wind, as it went
Creeping along from tent to tent,
And seeming to whisper, "All is well!"
A moment only he feels the spell
Of the place and the hour, and the secret
    dread

Of the lonely belfry and the dead;
For suddenly all his thoughts are bent
On a shadowy something far away,
Where the river widens to meet the bay,—
A line of black that bends and floats
On the rising tide, like a bridge of boats.

Meanwhile, impatient to mount and ride,
Booted and spurred, with a heavy stride
On the opposite shore walked Paul Revere.
Now he patted his horse's side,
Now gazed at the landscape far and near,
Then, impetuous, stamped the earth,
And turned and tightened his saddle girth;
But mostly he watched with eager search
The belfry's tower of the Old North Church,
As it rose above the graves on the hill,
Lonely and spectral and sombre and still.
And lo! as he looks, on the belfry height
A glimmer, and then a gleam of light!
He springs to the saddle, the bridle he turns,
But lingers and gazes, till full on his sight
A second lamp in the belfry burns!

A hurry of hoofs in a village street,
A shape in the moonlight, a bulk in the dark,

And beneath, from the pebbles, in passing, a
      spark
Struck out by a steed flying fearless and fleet;
That was all! And yet, through the gloom and
      the light,
The fate of a nation was riding that night;
And the spark struck out by that steed, in his
      flight,
Kindled the land into flame with its heat.
He has left the village and mounted the
      steep,
And beneath him, tranquil and broad and
      deep,
Is the Mystic, meeting the ocean tides;
And under the alders that skirt its edge,
Now soft on the sand, now loud on the ledge,
Is heard the tramp of his steed as he rides.

It was twelve by the village clock,
When he crossed the bridge into Medford
      town.
He heard the crowing of the cock,
And the barking of the farmer's dog,
And he felt the damp of the river fog,
That rises after the sun goes down.

It was one by the village clock,
When he galloped into Lexington.
He saw the gilded weathercock
Swim in the moonlight as he passed,
And the meeting-house windows, blank and
      bare,
Gaze at him with a spectral glare,
As if they already stood aghast
At the bloody work they would look upon.

It was two by the village clock,
When he came to the bridge in Concord
      town.
He heard the bleating of the flock,
And the twitter of birds among the trees,
And felt the breath of the morning breeze
Blowing over the meadows brown.
And one was safe and asleep in his bed
Who at the bridge would be first to fall,
Who that day would be lying dead,
Pierced by a British musket-ball.

You know the rest. In books you have read,
How the British Regulars fired and fled,—
How the farmers gave them ball for ball,

From behind each fence and farmyard wall,
Chasing the redcoats down the lane,
Then crossing the fields to emerge again
Under the trees at the turn of the road,
And only pausing to fire and load.
So through the night rode Paul Revere;
And so through the night went his cry of
      alarm
To every Middlesex village and farm,—
A cry of defiance, and not of fear,
A voice in the darkness, a knock at the door,
And a word that shall echo for evermore!
For, borne on the night-wind of the Past,
Through all our history, to the last,
In the hour of darkness and peril and need,
The people will waken and listen to hear
The hurrying hoof-beats of that steed,
And the midnight message of Paul Revere.

— HENRY WADSWORTH
LONGFELLOW

❧

The Marines' Hymn

From the Halls of Montezuma to the shores of
    Tripoli,
We fight our country's battles in the air, on
    land and sea,
First to fight for right and freedom
And to keep our honor clean,
We are proud to claim the title
Of United States Marines.

Our flag's unfurled to ev'ry breeze
From dawn to setting sun
We have fought in ev'ry clime and place
Where we could take a gun
In the snow of far-off northern lands
And in sunny tropic scenes
You will find us always on the job
The United States Marines.

Here's health to you and to our corps
Which we are proud to serve
In many a strife we've fought for life
And never lost our nerve
If the Army and the Navy
Ever look on heaven's scenes
They will find the streets are guarded
By United States Marines.

— ANONYMOUS

Battle Hymn of the Republic

Mine eyes have seen the glory of the coming
    of the Lord:
He is trampling out the vintage where the
    grapes of wrath are stored;
He hath loosed the fateful lightning of his
    terrible swift sword;
    His truth is marching on.

CHORUS:

    Glory! glory! Hallelujah!
    Glory! glory! Hallelujah!
    Glory! glory! Hallelujah!
      His truth is marching on!

I have seen him in the watch-fires of a
    hundred circling camps;
They have builded him an altar in the
    evening dews and damps;
I can read his righteous sentence by the dim
    and flaring lamps:
    His day is marching on.

I have read a fiery gospel, writ in burnished
    rows of steel:

"As ye deal with my contemners, so with you
        my grace shall deal;
Let the Hero, born of woman, crush the
        serpent with his heel,
        Since God is marching on."

He has sounded forth the trumpet that shall
        never call retreat;
He is sifting out the hearts of men before his
        judgment-seat;
Oh, be swift, my soul, to answer him! be
        jubilant, my feet!
        Our God is marching on.

In the beauty of the lilies Christ was born
        across the sea,
With a glory in his bosom that transfigures
        you and me:
As he died to make men holy, let us die to
        make men free,
        While God is marching on.

— JULIA WARD HOWE

❧

When Johnny Comes Marching Home

When Johnny comes marching home again,
Hurrah! Hurrah!
We'll give him a hearty welcome then,
Hurrah! Hurrah!
The men will cheer, and the boys will shout,
The ladies they will all turn out,
And we'll all feel gay
When Johnny comes marching home.

The old church bell will peal with joy,
Hurrah! Hurrah!
To welcome home our darling boy,
Hurrah! Hurrah!
The village lads and lassies say
With roses they will strew the way,
And we'll all feel gay
When Johnny comes marching home.

Get ready for the Jubilee,
Hurrah! Hurrah!

We'll give the hero three times three,
Hurrah! Hurrah!
The laurel wreath is ready now
To place upon his loyal brow
And we'll all feel gay
When Johnny comes marching home.

— PATRICK S. GILMORE

Shiloh

A Requiem (April 1862)

Skimming lightly, wheeling still,
  The swallows fly low
Over the field in clouded days,
  The forest-field of Shiloh—
Over the field where April rain
Solaced the parched one stretched in pain
Through the pause of night
That followed the Sunday fight
  Around the church of Shiloh—
The church so lone, the log-built one,
That echoed to many a parting groan
    And natural prayer
  Of dying foemen mingled there—
Foemen at morn, but friends at eve—
  Fame or country least their care:
(What like a bullet can undeceive!)
  But now they lie low,
While over them the swallows skim,
  And all is hushed at Shiloh.

— HERMAN MELVILLE

Mademoiselle from Armentières

Mademoiselle from Armentières, parley voo,
Mademoiselle from Armentières, parley voo,
  Mademoiselle from Armentières,
  She hasn't been kissed in forty years,
Hinky, dinky, parley voo.

Mademoiselle from Armentières, parley voo,
Mademoiselle from Armentières, parley voo,
  She had a form like the back of a hack,
  When she cried the tears ran down her
      back,
Hinky, dinky, parley voo.

Mademoiselle from Armentières, parley voo,
Mademoiselle from Armentières, parley voo,
  She never could hold the love of a man
  'Cause she took her baths in a talcum can,
Hinky, dinky, parley voo.

Mademoiselle from Armentières, parley voo,
Mademoiselle from Armentières, parley voo,
  She had four chins, her knees would knock,
  And her face would stop a coo-coo clock.
Hinky, dinky, parley voo.

Mademoiselle from Armentières, parley voo,
Mademoiselle from Armentières, parley voo,
    She could guzzle a barrel of sour wine,
    And eat a hog without peeling the rine,
Hinky, dinky, parley voo.

Mademoiselle from Armentières, parley voo,
Mademoiselle from Armentières, parley voo,
    She could beg a franc, a drink, a meal,
    But it wasn't because of sex appeal,
Hinky, dinky, parley voo.

— ANONYMOUS

Oh! Susanna

I come from Alabama,
Wid my banjo on my knee,
I'm g'wan to Louisiana,
My true love for to see.
It rain'd all night the day I left,
The weather it was dry;
The sun so hot I froze to death;
Susanna, don't you cry.

CHORUS:

Oh! Susanna,
Don't you cry for me,
I come from Alabama
Wid my banjo on my knee.

I jumped aboard de telegraph,
And trabbeled down de ribber,
De lectric fluid magnified,
And killed five hundred nigger;

De bullgine bust, de horse run off,
I really thought I'd die;
I shut my eyes to hold my breath;
Susanna, don't you cry.

I had a dream de udder night,
When eb'ryting was still;
I thought I saw Susanna,
A coming down de hill;
De buckwheat-cake was in her
      mouth,
De tear was in her eye;
Says I, I'm coming from de South,
Susanna, don't you cry.

I soon will be in New Orleans,
And den I'll look all round,
And when I find Susanna,
I'll fall upon the ground.
But if I do not find her,
Dis darkey'l surely die;
And when I'm dead and buried,
Susanna, don't you cry.

— STEPHEN FOSTER

The Man on the Flying Trapeze

Oh, the girl that I loved she was handsome,
I tried all I knew her to please,
But I couldn't please her a quarter as well
As the man on the flying trapeze.

CHORUS:

*Oh, he flies through the air with the greatest
of ease,*
This daring young man on the flying trapeze.
*His figure is handsome, all girls he can
please,*
And my love he purloined her away.

Last night as usual I went to her home.
There sat her old father and mother alone.
I asked for my love and they soon made it
known
That she-e had flown away.

She packed up her box and eloped in the
night,
To go-o with him at his ease.
He lowered her down from a four-story flight
By means of his flying trapeze.

He took her to town and he dreseed her in
      tights,
That he-e might live at his ease.
He ordered her up to the tent's awful height,
To appear on the flying trapeze.

Now she flies through the air with the
      greatest of ease,
This daring young girl on the flying trapeze.
Her figure as handsome all men she can
      please,
And my love is purloined away.

Once I was happy but now I'm forlorn,
Like an old coat that is tattered and torn,
Left to this wide world to fret and to mourn,
Betrayed by a maid in her teens.

— Anonymous

Poor Lonesome Cowboy

I ain't got no father,
I ain't got no father,
I ain't got no father
To buy the clothes I wear.

   I'm a poor, lonesome cowboy,
   I'm a poor, lonesome cowboy,
   I'm a poor, lonesome cowboy
   And a long ways from home.

I ain't got no mother,
I ain't got no mother,
I ain't got no mother
To mend the clothes I wear.

I ain't got no sister,
I ain't got no sister,
I ain't got no sister
To go and play with me.

I ain't got no brother,
I ain't got no brother,
I ain't got no brother
To drive the steers with me.

I ain't got no sweetheart,
I ain't got no sweetheart,
I ain't got no sweetheart
To sit and talk with me.

I'm a poor, lonesome cowboy,
I'm a poor, lonesome cowboy,
I'm a poor, lonesome cowboy
And a long ways from home.

— ANONYMOUS

Dixie

[THE ORIGINAL VERSION]

I wish I was in de land ob cotton,
Old times dar am not forgotten;
   Look away, look away, look away,
     Dixie land!
In Dixie land whar I was born in,
Early on one frosty mornin',
   Look away, look away, look away,
     Dixie land!

CHORUS:

Den I wish I was in Dixie! Hooray! Hooray!
In Dixie's land we'll take our stand, to lib an'
    die in Dixie,
Away, away, away down south in Dixie!
Away, away, away down south in Dixie!

Old missus marry Will de weaber,
William was a gay deceaber.
When he put his arm around 'er,
Looked as fierce as a forty-pounder.

His face was sharp as a butcher cleaber,
But dat did not seem to greab 'er;
Will run away, missus took a decline, O,
Her face was the color of bacon rhine, O.

While missus libbed, she libbed in clover,
When she died, she died all over;
How could she act de foolish part,
An' marry a man to break her heart?

Buckwheat cakes an' stony batter
Makes you fat or a little fatter;
Here's a health to de next old missus,
An' all de gals dat want to kiss us.

Now if you want to drive 'way sorrow,
Come an' hear dis song to-morrow;
Den hoe it down an' scratch your grabble,
To Dixie's land I'm bound to trabble.

— DANIEL DECATUR EMMETT

The Cowboy's Lament

As I walked out in the streets of Laredo,
As I walked out in Laredo one day,
I spied a poor cowboy wrapped up in white
    linen,
Wrapped up in white linen as cold as the
    clay.

"Oh, beat the drum slowly and play the fife
    lowly,
Play the dead march as you carry me along;
Take me to the green valley, there lay the sod
    o'er me,
For I'm a young cowboy and I know I've
    done wrong.

"I see by your outfit that you are a cowboy"—
These words he did say as I boldly stepped
    by.
"Come sit down beside me and hear my sad
    story;
I am shot in the breast and I know I must die.

"Let sixteen gamblers come handle my coffin,
Let sixteen cowboys come sing me a song.

Take me to the graveyard and lay the sod o'er
    me,
For I'm a poor cowboy and I know I've done
    wrong.

"My friends and relations they live in the
    Nation,
They know not where their boy has gone.
He first came to Texas and hired to a
    ranchman,
Oh, I'm a young cowboy and I know I've
    done wrong.

"It was once in the saddle I used to go
    dashing;
It was once in the saddle I used to go gay;
First to the dram-house and then to the card-
    house;
Got shot in the breast and I am dying today.

"Get six jolly cowboys to carry my coffin;
Get six pretty maidens to bear up my pall.
Put bunches of roses all over my coffin,
Put roses to deaden the sods as they fall.

"Then swing your rope slowly and rattle your
    spurs lowly,
And give a wild whoop as you carry me
    along;
And in the grave throw me and roll the sod
    o'e me
For I'm a young cowboy and I know I've
    done wrong.

"Oh, bury beside me my knife and six-
    shooter,
My spurs on my heel, my rifle by my side,
And over my coffin put a bottle of brandy
That the cowboys may drink as they carry me
    along.

"Go bring me a cup, a cup of cold water,
To cool my parched lips," the cowboy then
    said;
Before I returned his soul had departed,   .
And gone to the round-up—the cowboy was
    dead.

We beat the drum slowly and played the fife
    lowly,
And bitterly wept as we bore him along;

For we all loved our comrade, so brave,
    young, and handsome,
We all loved our comrade although he'd done
    wrong.

Where men lived raw, in the desert's maw,
And hell was nothing to shun;
Where they buried 'em neat, without
    preacher or sheet,
And writ on their foreheads, crude but
    sweet,
"This Jasper was slow with a gun."

— ANONYMOUS

Sweet Betsey from Pike

Oh, don't you remember sweet Betsey from
    Pike,
Who crossed the big mountains with her
    lover Ike,
With two yoke of cattle, a large yellow dog,
A tall shanghai rooster and one spotted hog.

CHORUS:

Singing, goodbye, Pike County, farewell for
awhile,
We'll come back again when we've panned
out our pile,
Singing tooral lal, looral lal, looral lal lay,
Singing tooral lal, looral lal, looral lal lay.

One evening quite early they camped on the
Platte,
'Twas near by the road on a green shady flat,
Where Betsey, sore-footed, lay down to
repose,
While with wonder Ike gazed on his Pike
County rose.

Their wagon broke down with a terrible
crash,
And out on the prairie rolled all kinds of
trash;
A few little baby clothes done up with great
care—
'Twas rather suspicious, though all on the
square.

The shanghai ran off and the cattle all died;
That morning the last piece of bacon was
     fried;
Poor Ike was discouraged, and Betsey got
     mad,
The dog drooped his tail and looked
     wondrously sad.

They stopped at Salt Lake to inquire the way,
When Brigham declared that sweet Betsey
     should stay;
But Betsey got frightened and ran like a deer,
While Brigham stood pawing the ground like
     a steer.

They soon reached the desert, where Betsey
     gave out,
And down in the sand she lay rolling about;
While Ike, half distracted, looked on with
     surprise,
Saying, "Betsey, get up, you'll get sand in
     your eyes."

Sweet Betsey got up in a great deal of pain,
Declared she'd go back to Pike County again;

But Ike gave a sigh, and they fondly
      embraced,
And they traveled along with his arm round
      her waist.

They suddenly stopped on a very high hill,
With wonder looked down upon old
      Placerville;
Ike sighed when he said, and he cast his eyes
      down,
"Sweet Betsey, my darling, we've got to
      Hangtown."

Long Ike and sweet Betsey attended a dance,
Ike wore a pair of his Pike County pants;
Sweet Betsey was covered with ribbons and
      rings;
Says Ike, "You're an angel, but where are
      your wings?"

A miner said, "Betsey, will you dance with
      me?"
"I will that, old hoss, if you don't make too
      free;
But don't dance me hard, do you want to
      know why?
Dog on you! I'm chock full of strong alkali!"

This Pike County couple got married, of
    course,
And Ike became jealous—obtained a divorce;
Sweet Betsey, well satisfied, said with a
    shout,
"Goodbye, you big lummox, I'm glad you've
    backed out!"

— ANONYMOUS

The Big Rock Candy Mountains

One evening as the sun went down
And the jungle fire was burning,
Down the track came a hobo hiking.
And he said, "Boys, I'm not turning,
I'm headed for a land that's far away,
Beside the crystal fountains,
So come with me, we'll go and see
The Big Rock Candy Mountains."

In the Big Rock Candy Mountains,
There's a land that's fair and bright,
Where the handouts grow on bushes,
And you sleep out every night.

Where the boxcars all are empty,
And the sun shines every day
On the birds and the bees,
And the cigarette trees,
And the lemonade springs
Where the Bluebird sings
In the Big Rock Candy Mountains.

In the Big Rock Candy Mountains
All the cops have wooden legs,
And the bulldogs all have rubber teeth,
And the hens lay softboiled eggs.
There the farmer's trees are full of fruit,
And the barns are full of hay,
And I'm bound to go
Where there ain't no snow,
And the rain don't fall,
And the wind don't blow
In the Big Rock Candy Mountains.

In the Big Rock Candy Mountains
You never change your socks,
And the little streams of alcohol
Come a-trickling down the rocks.
There ain't no shorthandled shovels,
No axes, spades, or picks,
And I'm bound to stay

Where they sleep all day,
Where they hung the Turk
That invented work
In the Big Rock Candy Mountains.

In the Big Rock Candy Mountains
All the jails are made of tin,
And you can walk right out again
As soon as you are in.
Where the brakemen have to tip their hats,
And the railroad bulls are blind,
There's a lake of stew,
And a gin lake, too,
You can paddle all around 'em
In a big canoe
In the Big Rock Candy Mountains.

— ANONYMOUS

Casey at the Bat

The outlook wasn't brilliant for the Mudville
    nine that day;
The score stood four to two with but one
    inning more to play.

And then, when Cooney died at first, and
       Barrows did the same,
A sickly silence fell upon the patrons of the
       game.

A straggling few got up to go in deep despair.
       The rest
Clung to that hope which springs eternal in
       the human breast;
They thought, If only Casey could but get a
       whack at that
We'd put up even money now, with Casey at
       the bat.

But Flynn preceded Casey, as did also Jimmy
       Blake,
And the former was a lulu and the latter was a
       cake;
So upon that stricken multitude grim
       melancholy sat,
For there seemed but little chance of Casey's
       getting to the bat.

But Flynn let drive a single, to the
       wonderment of all,
And Blake, the much despised, tore the cover
       off the ball;

And when the dust had lifted, and men saw
    what had occurred,
There was Jimmy safe at second, and Flynn
    a-hugging third.

Then from five thousand throats and more
    there rose a lusty yell;
It rumbled through the valley, it rattled in the
    dell;
It knocked upon the mountain and recoiled
    upon the flat,
For Casey, mighty Casey, was advancing to
    the bat.

There was ease in Casey's manner as he
    stepped into his place;
There was pride in Casey's bearing and a
    smile on Casey's face.
And when, responding to the cheers, he
    lightly doffed his hat,
No stranger in the crowd could doubt 'twas
    Casey at the bat.

Ten thousand eyes were on him as he rubbed
    his hands with dirt,
Five thousand tongues applauded when he
    wiped them on his shirt;

Then while the writhing pitcher ground the
     ball into his hip,
Defiance gleamed from Casey's eye, a sneer
     curled Casey's lip.

And now the leather-covered sphere came
     hurtling through the air,
And Casey stood a-watching it in haughty
     grandeur there.
Close by the sturdy batsman the ball
     unheeded sped;
"That ain't my style," said Casey. "Strike
     one," the umpire said.

From the benches, black with people, there
     went up a muffled roar,
Like the beating of the storm waves on a
     stern and distant shore.
"Kill him! Kill the umpire!" shouted someone
     on the stand;
And it's likely they'd have killed him had not
     Casey raised his hand.

With a smile of Christian charity great
     Casey's visage shone;
He stilled the rising tumult, he bade the
     game go on;

He signaled to the pitcher, and once more the
    spheroid flew;
But Casey still ignored it, and the umpire
    said, "Strike two."

"Fraud!" cried the maddened thousands, and
    echo answered "Fraud!"
But one scornful look from Casey and the
    audience was awed;
They saw his face grow stern and cold, they
    saw his muscles strain,
And they knew that Casey wouldn't let that
    ball go by again.

The sneer is gone from Casey's lip, his teeth
    are clenched in hate,
He pounds with cruel violence his bat upon
    the plate;
And now the pitcher holds the ball, and now
    he lets it go,
And now the air is shattered by the force of
    Casey's blow.

Oh, somewhere in this favored land the sun is
    shining bright,
The band is playing somewhere, and
    somewhere hearts are light;

And somewhere men are laughing, and
    somewhere children shout,
But there is no joy in Mudville—mighty
    Casey has struck out.

— ERNEST LAWRENCE THAYER

Bill Bailey, Won't You Please Come Home?

On one summer's day,
Sun was shining fine,
De lady love of old Bill Bailey
Was hanging clothes on de line
In her back yard,
And weeping hard;
She married a B. and O. brakeman,
Dat took and throw'd her down.
Bellering like a prune-fed calf,
Wid a big gang hanging 'round;
And to dat crowd,
She yelled out loud:

*"Won't you come home, Bill Bailey, won't
     you come home?"*
She moans de whole day long.
"I'll do de cooking, darling, I'll pay de rent;
I knows I've done you wrong.
'Member dat rainy eve dat I drove you out
Wid nothing but a fine tooth comb!
I know I'se to blame, well ain't dat a shame?
Bill Bailey, won't you please come home?"

Bill drove by dat door
In an automobile,
A great big diamond, coach and footman,
Hear dat big wench squeal:
"He's all alone,"
I heard her groan;
She hollered thro' dat door:
"Bill Bailey, is you sore?
Stop a minute won't you listen to me?
Won't I see you no more?"
Bill winked his eye,
As he heard her cry: [*Repeat refrain*]

— HUGHIE CANNON

281

A Poem on Table Manners, Used by a Shaker Community in 1868

We found of these bounties
    Which heaven does give,
That some live to eat,
    And that some eat to live—
That some think of nothing
    But pleasing the taste,
And care very little
    How much they do waste.

Tho' heaven has bless'd us
    With plenty of food;
Bread, butter and honey,
    And all that is good;
We loathe to see mixtures
    Where gentle folk dine,
Which scarcely look fit
    For the poultry or swine.

We often find left,
    On the same china dish,
Meat, apple-sauce, pickle,
    Brown bread and minced fish;

Another's replenish'd
  With butter and cheese;
With pie, cake and toast,
  Perhaps added to these

— ANONYMOUS

Hometown Piece for Messrs. Alston and Reese

To the tune:
"Li'l baby, don't say a word: Mama goin' to
     buy you a mockingbird.
Bird don't sing: Mama goin' to sell it and buy
     a brass ring."

"Millennium," yes; "pandemonium"!
Roy Campanella leaps high. Dodgerdom

crowned, had Johnny Podres on the mound.
Buzzie Bavasi and the Press gave ground;

the team slapped, mauled, and asked the
      Yankees' match,
"How did you feel when Sandy Amoros made
      the catch?"

"I said to myself"—pitcher for all innings—
"as I walked back to the mound I said,
      'Everything's

getting better and better,' " (Zest: they've
      zest.
" 'Hope springs eternal in the Brooklyn
      breast.' "

And would the Dodger Band in 8, row 1,
      relax
if they saw the collector of income tax?

Ready with a tune if that should occur:
"Why Not Take All of Me—All of Me, Sir?")

Another series. Round-tripper Duke at bat,
"Four hundred feet from home-plate"; more
      like that.

A neat bunt, please; a cloud-breaker, a drive
like Jim Gilliam's great big one. Hope's alive.

Homered, flied out, fouled? Our "stylish
      stout"
so nimble Campanella will have him out.

A-squat in double-headers four hundred
      times a day,
he says that in a measure the pleasure is the
      pay:

catcher to pitcher, a nice easy throw
almost as if he'd just told it to go.

Willie Mays should be a Dodger. He
      should—
a lad for Roger Craig and Clem Labine
      to elude;

but you have an omen, pennant-winning
      Peewee,
on which we are looking superstitiously.

Ralph Branca has Preacher Roe's number;
      recall?
and there's Don Bessent; he can really fire
      the ball.

As for Gil Hodges, in custody of first—
"He'll do it by himself." Now a specialist—
      versed

in an extension reach far into the box seats—
he lengthens up, leans and gloves the ball.
      He defeats

expectation by a whisker. The modest star,
irked by one misplay, is no hero by a hair;

in a strikeout slaughter when what could
      matter more,
he lines a homer to the signboard and has
      changed the score.

Then for his nineteenth season, a home run—
with four of six runs batted in—Carl Furillo's
      the big gun;

almost dehorned the foe—has fans dancing in
      delight.
Jake Pitler and his Playground "get a
      Night"—

Jake, that hearty man, made heartier by a
      harrier
who can bat as well as field—Don Demeter.

Shutting them out for nine innings—hitter
      too—
Carl Erskine leaves Cimoli nothing to do.

Take off the goat-horns, Dodgers, that egret
which two very fine base-stealers can offset.

You've got plenty: Jackie Robinson
and Campy and big Newk, and Dodgerdom
      again
watching everything you do. You won last
      year. Come on.

— MARIANNE MOORE

Tableau

Locked arm in arm they cross the way,
  The black boy and the white,
The golden splendor of the day,
  The sable pride of night.

From lowered blinds the dark folk stare,
  And here the fair folk talk,
Indignant that these two should dare
  In unison to walk.

Oblivious to look and word
  They pass, and see no wonder
That lightning brilliant as a sword
  Should blaze the path of thunder.

— Countee Cullen

Waltz Me Around Again, Willie

Willie Fitzgibbons who used to sell ribbons,
And stood up all day on his feet,
Grew very spooney on Madeline Mooney,
Who'd rather be dancing than eat.
Each evening she'd tag him, to some dance
    hall drag him,
And when the band started to play,
She'd up like a silly and grab tired Willie,
Steer him on the floor and she'd say:

CHORUS:

"Waltz me around again, Willie, a-round,
    a-round, a-round,
The music it's dreamy, it's peaches and
    creamy,
Oh! don't let my feet touch the ground.
I feel like a ship on an ocean of joy,
I just want to holler out loud, 'Ship ahoy!'
Oh, waltz me around again, Willie, a-round,
    a-round, a-round."

Willie De Vere was a dry goods cashier,
At his desk he would sit all the day,
Till his doctor advised him to start exercising,

Or else he would soon fade away.
One night this poor looney met Madeline
      Mooney,
Fitzgibbons then shouted with joy,
"She's a good health regainer, you've got a
      great trainer,
Just wait till she hollers, my boy. [*Repeat
      chorus.*]

— WILL D. COBB

Take Me Out to the Ball Game

Take me out to the ball game,
Take me out with the crowd.
Buy me some peanuts and Cracker Jack
I don't care if I never get back.
Let me root, root, root, for the home town,
If they don't win it's a shame,
For it's one, two, three strikes you're out
At the old ball game.

— JACK NORWORTH

Country Life/
City Life

Up at a Villa—Down in the City

(As Distinguished by an Italian Person of Quality)

Had I but plenty of money, money enough
    and to spare,
The house for me, no doubt, were a house in
    the city-square;
Ah, such a life, such a life, as one leads at the
    window there!

Something to see, by Bacchus, something to
    hear, at least!
There, the whole day long, one's life is a
    perfect feast;
While up at a villa one lives, I maintain it, no
    more than a beast.

Well now, look at our villa! stuck like the
    horn of a bull
Just on a mountain-edge as bare as the
    creature's skull,
Save a mere shag of a bush with hardly a leaf
    to pull!
—I scratch my own, sometimes, to see if the
    hair's turned wool.

But the city, oh the city—the square with the
    houses! Why?
They are stone-faced, white as a curd, there's
    something to take the eye!
Houses in four straight lines, not a single
    front awry;
You watch who crosses and gossips, who
    saunters, who hurries by;
Green blinds, as a matter of course, to draw
    when the sun gets high;
And the shops with fanciful signs which are
    painted properly.

What of a villa? Though winter be over in
    March by rights,
'Tis May perhaps ere the snow shall have
    withered well off the heights:
You've the brown ploughed land before,
    where the oxen steam and wheeze,
And the hills over-smoked behind by the
    faint gray olive-trees.

Is it better in May, I ask you? You've summer
    all at once;
In a day he leaps complete with a few strong
    April suns.

'Mid the sharp short emerald wheat, scarce
      risen three fingers well,
The wild tulip, at the end of its tube, blows
      out its great red bell
Like a thin clear bubble of blood, for the
      children to pick and sell.

Is it ever hot in the square? There's a
      fountain to spout and splash!
In the shade it sings and springs: in the shine
      such foam-bows flash
On the horses with curling fish-tails, that
      prance and paddle and pash
Round the lady atop in her conch—fifty
      gazers do not abash,
Though all that she wears is some weeds
      round her waist in a sort of sash.

All the year long at the villa, nothing to see
      though you linger,
Except yon cypress that points like death's
      lean lifted fore-finger.
Some think fireflies pretty, when they mix i'
      the corn and mingle,
Or thrid the stinking hemp till the stalks of it
      seem a-tingle.

Late August or early September, the stunning
    cicala is shrill,
And the bees keep their tiresome whine
    round the resinous firs on the hill.
Enough of the seasons,—I spare you the
    months of the fever and chill.

Ere you open your eyes in the city, the
    blessed church-bells begin:
No sooner the bells leave off than the
    diligence rattles in:
You get the pick of the news, and it costs you
    never a pin.
By-and-by there's the travelling doctor gives
    pills, lets blood, draws teeth;
Or the Pulcinello-trumpet breaks up the
    market beneath.
At the post-office such a scene-picture—the
    new play, piping hot!
And a notice how, only this morning, three
    liberal thieves were shot.
Above it, behold the Archbishop's most
    fatherly of rebukes,
And beneath, with his crown and his lion,
    some little new law of the Duke's!
Or a sonnet with flowery marge, to the
    Reverend Don So-and-so,

Who is Dante, Boccaccio, Petrarca, Saint
      Jerome, and Cicero,
"And moreover" (the sonnet goes rhyming),
      "the skirts of Saint Paul has reached,
Having preached us those six Lent-lectures
      more unctuous than ever he preached."
Noon strikes,—here sweeps the procession!
      our Lady borne smiling and smart
With a pink gauze gown all spangles, and
      seven swords stuck in her heart!
Bang-whang-whang goes the drum, *tootle-te-*
      tootle the fife;
No keeping one's haunches still: it's the
      greatest pleasure in life.

But bless you, it's dear—it's dear! fowls,
      wine, at double the rate.
They have clapped a new tax upon salt, and
      what oil pays passing the gate
It's a horror to think of. And so, the villa for
      me, not the city!
Beggars can scarcely be choosers: but still—
      ah, the pity, the pity!
Look, two and two go the priests, then the
      monks with cowls and sandals,

And the penitents dressed in white shirts,
    a-holding the yellow candles;
One, he carries a flag up straight, and another
    a cross with handles,
And the Duke's guard brings up the rear, for
    the better prevention of scandals:
Bang-whang-whang goes the drum, *tootle-te-*
    tootle the fife.
Oh, a day in the city-square, there is no such
    pleasure in life!

— ROBERT BROWNING

My Heart's in the Highlands

Farewell to the Highlands, farewell to the
    North,
The birth-place of valor, the country of worth!
Wherever I wander, wherever I rove,
The hills of the Highlands for ever I love.

    My heart's in the Highlands, my heart is
        not here,
    My heart's in the Highlands a-chasing the
        deer,

A-chasing the wild deer and following the
    roe—
My heart's in the Highlands, wherever I go.

Farewell to the mountains high-covered with
    snow,
Farewell to the straths and green valleys
    below,
Farewell to the forests and wild-hanging
    woods,
Farewell to the torrents and loud-pouring
    floods!

My heart's in the Highlands, my heart is
    not here;
My heart's in the Highlands a-chasing the
    deer,
A-chasing the wild deer and following the
    roe—
My heart's in the Highlands, wherever I
    go!

— Robert Burns

Home-Thoughts from Abroad

Oh, to be in England
Now that April's there,
And whoever wakes in England
Sees, some morning, unaware,
That the lowest boughs and the brush-wood
    sheaf
Round the elm-tree bole are in tiny leaf,
While the chaffinch sings on the orchard
    bough
In England—now!

And after April, when May follows,
And the whitethroat builds, and all the
    swallows—
Hark! where my blossomed pear-tree in the
    hedge
Leans to the field and scatters on the clover
Blossoms and dewdrops—at the bent-spray's
    edge—
That's the wise thrush; he sings each song
    twice over,
Lest you should think he never could
    recapture
The first fine careless rapture!

And though the fields look rough with hoary
      dew,
All will be gay when noontide wakes anew
The buttercups, the little children's dower,
—Far brighter than this gaudy melon-flower!

— ROBERT BROWNING

The Village Blacksmith

Under a spreading chestnut-tree
    The village smithy stands;
The smith, a mighty man is he,
    With large and sinewy hands;
And the muscles of his brawny arms
    Are strong as iron bands.

His hair is crisp, and black, and long,
    His face is like the tan;
His brow is wet with honest sweat,
    He earns whate'er he can,
And looks the whole world in the face,
    For he owes not any man.

Week in, week out, from morn till night,
    You can hear his bellows blow;
You can hear him swing his heavy sledge
    With measured beat and slow,
Like a sexton ringing the village bell,
    When the evening sun is low.

And children coming home from school
    Look in at the open door;
They love to see the flaming forge,
    And hear the bellows roar,
And catch the burning sparks that fly
    Like chaff from a threshing-floor.

He goes on Sunday to the church,
    And sits among his boys;
He hears the parson pray and preach,
    He hears his daughter's voice,
Singing in the village choir,
    And it makes his heart rejoice.

It sounds to him like her mother's voice,
    Singing in Paradise!
He needs must think of her once more,
    How in the grave she lies;
And with his hard, rough hand he wipes
    A tear out of his eyes.

Toiling,—rejoicing,—sorrowing,
  Onward through life he goes;
Each morning sees some task begin,
  Each evening sees its close;
Something attempted, something done,
  Has earned a night's repose.

Thanks, thanks to thee, my worthy friend,
  For the lesson thou hast taught!
Thus at the flaming forge of life
  Our fortunes must be wrought;
Thus on its sounding anvil shaped
  Each burning deed and thought!

— HENRY WADSWORTH
LONGFELLOW

The Old Oaken Bucket

How dear to my heart are the scenes of my
    childhood,
  When fond recollection presents them to
    view!
The orchard, the meadow, the deep-tangled
    wildwood,

And every loved spot which my infancy
knew,
The wide-spreading pond and the mill which
stood by it,
The bridge and the rock where the cataract
fell;
The cot of my father, the dairy house nigh it,
And e'en the rude-bucket which hung in
the well.
The old oaken bucket, the iron-bound bucket,
The moss-covered bucket which hung in the
well.

That moss-covered vessel I hail as a treasure;
For often at noon, when returned from the
field,
I found it the source of an exquisite pleasure,
The purest and sweetest that nature can
yield.
How ardent I seized it with hands that were
glowing!
And quick to the white-pebbled bottom it
fell;
Then soon, with the emblem of truth
overflowing,
And dripping with coolness it rose from the
well;

The old oaken bucket, the iron-bound bucket,
The moss-covered bucket, arose from the
    well.

How sweet from the green mossy brim to
        receive it,
    As poised on the curb, it inclined to my
        lips!
Not a full blushing goblet could tempt me to
        leave it,
    Though filled with the nectar that Jupiter
        sips.
And now, far removed from the loved
        situation,
    The tear of regret will intrusively swell,
As fancy reverts to my father's plantation,
    And sighs for the bucket which hangs in
        the well;
The old oaken bucket, the iron-bound bucket,
The moss-covered bucket which hangs in the
    well.

— SAMUEL WOODWORTH

On Being Brought from Africa to America

'Twas mercy brought me from my *Pagan* land.
Taught my benighted soul to understand
That there's a God, that there's a *Saviour* too:
Once I redemption neither sought nor knew.
Some view our race with scornful eye,
"Their color is a diabolic die."
Remember, Christians, Negroes, black as
    Cain,
May be refined, and join th' angelic train.

— PHYLLIS WHEATLEY

Dance the Boatman

The boatman he can dance and sing
And he's the lad for any old thing.
   Dance the boatman, dance!
   Dance the boatman, dance!
He'll dance all night on his toes so light
And go down to his boat in the morning.
   Hooraw the boatman, ho!
   Spends his money with the gals ashore!
   Hooraw the boatman, ho!
   Rolling down the Ohio!

From Louisville down the Ohio,
He's known wherever them boats do go,
   Dance the boatman, dance!
   Dance the boatman, dance!
He'll drink and dance and kiss them all,
And away in his boat in the morning.
   Hooraw the boatman, ho!
   Spends his money with the girls ashore!
   Hooraw the boatman, ho!
   Rolling down the Ohio!

The girls all wait for boatman Bill,
For he's the one they all love still,

Dance the boatman, dance!
Dance the boatman, dance!
He'll buy them drinks and swing them high,
And leave in his boat in the morning.
    Hooraw the boatman, ho!
    Spends his money with the gals ashore!
    Hooraw the boatman, ho!
    Rolling down the Ohio!

— ANONYMOUS

Out Where the West Begins

Out where the handclasp's a little stronger,
Out where the smile dwells a little longer,
    That's where the West begins;
Out where the sun is a little brighter,
Where the snows that fall are a trifle whiter,
Where the bonds of home are a wee bit
        tighter,—
    That's where the West begins.

Out where the skies are a trifle bluer,
Out where friendship's a little truer,
  That's where the West begins;
Out where a fresher breeze is blowing,
Where there's laughter in every streamlet
      flowing,
Where there's more of reaping and less of
      sowing,—
  That's where the West begins.

Out where the world is in the making,
Where fewer hearts in despair are aching,
  That's where the West begins;
Where there's more of singing and less of
      sighing,
Where there's more of giving and less of
      buying,
And a man makes friends without half
      trying—
  That's where the West begins.

— ARTHUR CHAPMAN

London

I wander through each chartered street,
Near where the chartered Thames does flow,
And mark in every face I meet,
Marks of weakness, marks of woe.

In every cry of every man,
In every infant's cry of fear,
In every voice, in every ban,
The mind-forged manacles I hear.

How the chimney-sweeper's cry
Every blackening church appalls;
And the hapless soldier's sigh
Runs in blood down palace walls.

But most through midnight streets I hear
How the youthful harlot's curse
Blasts the new-born infant's tear,
And blights with plagues the marriage hearse.

— WILLIAM BLAKE

Harlem Hopscotch

One foot down, then hop! It's hot.
  Good things for the ones that's got.
Another jump, now to the left.
  Everybody for hisself.

In the air, now both feet down.
  Since you black, don't stick around.
Food is gone, the rent is due,
  Curse and cry and then jump two.

All the people out of work,
  Hold for three, then twist and jerk.
Cross the line, they count you out.
  That's what hopping's all about.

Both feet flat, the game is done.
They think I lost. I think I won.

— MAYA ANGELOU

❧

Chicago

Hog Butcher for the World,
Tool maker, Stacker of Wheat,
Player with Railroads and the Nation's
      Freight Handler;
Stormy, husky, brawling,
City of the Big Shoulders:

They tell me you are wicked and I believe
      them, for I have seen your painted
      women under the gas lamps luring the
      farm boys.
And they tell me you are crooked and I
      answer: Yes, it is true I have seen the
      gunman kill and go free to kill again.
And they tell me you are brutal and my reply
      is: On the faces of women and children
      I have seen the marks of wanton
      hunger.
And having answered so I turn once more to
      those who sneer at this my city, and I
      give them back the sneer and say to
      them:

Come and show me another city with lifted
      head singing so proud to be alive and
      coarse and strong and cunning.
Flinging magnetic curses amid the toil of
      piling job on job, here is a tall bold
      slugger set vivid against the little soft
      cities;
Fierce as a dog with tongue lapping for
      action, cunning as a savage pitted
      against the wilderness,
         Bareheaded,
         Shoveling,
         Wrecking,
         Planning,
         Building, breaking, rebuilding,
Under the smoke, dust all over his mouth,
      laughing with white teeth,
Under the terrible burden of destiny laughing
      as a young man laughs,
Laughing even as an ignorant fighter laughs
      who has never lost a battle,
Bragging and laughing that under his wrist is
      the pulse,
And under his ribs the heart of the people,
         Laughing!

Laughing the stormy, husky, brawling
    laughter of Youth, half-naked,
    sweating, proud to be Hog Butcher,
    Tool Maker, Stacker of Wheat, Player
    with Railroads and Freight Handler to
    the Nation.

— CARL SANDBURG

Little Colt

Little colt, you can't help wobbling
On legs as long as those.
But you couldn't have them different—
Not even if you chose,

You have to have such lots of legs;
I'm glad you haven't more.
Just two are all I need. It must
Be hard to manage four.

I never saw legs any longer
Nor long ones any thinner.
But then you have to have long legs
So you can reach your dinner.

— ANONYMOUS

Woodchucking

I have chased fugacious woodchucks over
      many leagues of land,
But at last they've always vanished in a round
      hole in the sand;
And though I've been woodchucking many
      times—upon my soul—
I have never bagged my woodchuck, for he
      always found his hole.

I have chased my hot ambitions through the
      meadow white with flowers,
Chased them through the clover blossoms,
      chased them through the orchard
      bowers;

Chased them through the old scrub pastures
    till with weariness of soul
I at last have seen them vanish like a
    woodchuck in his hole.

But there's fun in chasing woodchucks, and
    I'll chase the vision still,
If it leads me through the dark pine woods
    and up the stony hill.
There's a glorious expectation that still
    lingers in my soul,
That some day I'll catch that woodchuck ere
    he slides into his hole.

— ANONYMOUS

To One Who Has Been Long in City Pent

To one who has been long in city pent,
    'Tis very sweet to look into the fair
    And open face of heaven,—to breathe a
       prayer
Full in the smile of the blue firmament.
Who is more happy, when, with hearts
    content,

Fatigued he sinks into some pleasant lair
Of wavy grass, and reads a debonair
And gentle tale of love and languishment?
Returning home at evening, with an ear
Catching the notes of Philomel,—an eye
Watching the sailing cloudlet's bright career,
He mourns that day so soon has glided
by:
E'en like the passage of an angel's tear
That falls through the clear ether silently.

— JOHN KEATS

The Tired Worker

O whisper, O my soul! The afternoon
Is waning into evening, whisper soft!
Peace, O my rebel heart! for soon the moon
From out its misty veil will swing aloft!
Be patient, weary body, soon the night
Will wrap thee gently in her sable sheet,
And with a leaden sigh thou wilt invite
To rest thy tired hands and aching feet.
The wretched day was theirs, the night is
      mine;
Come, tender sleep, and fold me to thy breast.
But what steals out the gray clouds red like
      wine?
O dawn! O dreaded dawn! O let me rest!
Weary my veins, my brain, my life! Have pity!
No! Once again the harsh, the ugly city.

— CLAUDE McKAY

My City

When I come down to sleep death's endless
      night,
The threshold of the unknown dark to cross,
What to me then will be the keenest loss,
When this bright world blurs on my fading
      sight?
Will it be that no more I shall see the trees
Or smell the flowers or hear the singing birds
Or watch the flashing streams or patient
      herds?
No, I am sure it will be none of these.

But, ah! Manhattan's sights and sounds, her
      smells,
Her crowds, her throbbing force, the thrill
      that comes
From being of her a part, her subtile spells,
Her shining towers, her avenues, her slums—
O God! the stark, unutterable pity,
To be dead, and never again behold my city!

— JAMES WELDON JOHNSON

Portraits

Jesse James

It was on a Wednesday night, the moon was
    shining bright,
  They robbed the Danville train.
And the people they did say, for many miles
    away,
  'Twas the outlaws Frank and Jesse James.

CHORUS:

Jesse had a wife to mourn him all her life,
  The children they are brave.
'Twas a dirty little coward shot Mister
    Howard,
  And laid Jesse James in his grave.

Jesse was a man was a friend to the poor,
  He never left a friend in pain.
And with his brother Frank he robbed the
    Chicago bank
  And then held up the Glendale train.

It was Robert Ford, the dirty little coward,
  I wonder how he does feel,

For he ate of Jesse's bread and he slept in
	Jesse's bed,
	Then he laid Jesse James in his grave.

It was his brother Frank that robbed the
	Gallatin bank,
	And carried the money from the town.
It was in this very place that they had a little
	race,
	For they shot Captain Sheets to the ground.

They went to the crossing not very far from
	there,
	And there they did the same;
And the agent on his knees he delivered up
	the keys
To the outlaws Frank and Jesse James.

It was on a Saturday night, Jesse was at home
	Talking to his family brave,
When the thief and the coward, little Robert
	Ford,
	Laid Jesse James in his grave.

How people held their breath when they
	heard of Jesse's death,
	And wondered how he ever came to die.

'Twas one of the gang, dirty Robert Ford,
   That shot Jesse James on the sly.

Jesse went to rest with his hand on his breast;
   He died with a smile on his face.
He was born one day in the county of Clay,
   And came from a solitary race.

— ANONYMOUS

An Elegy on That Glory of Her Sex, Mrs. Mary Blaize

Good people all, with one accord,
   Lament for Madame Blaize,
Who never wanted a good word—
   From those who spoke her praise.

The needy seldom pass'd her door,
   And always found her kind;
She freely lent to all the poor,—
   Who left a pledge behind.

She strove the neighbourhood to please,
    With manners wond'rous winning,
And never followed wicked ways,—
    Unless when she was sinning.

At church, in silks and satins new,
    With hoops of monstrous size,
She never slumber'd in her pew,—
    But when she shut her eyes.

Her love was sought, I do aver,
    By twenty beaux and more;
The king himself has followed her,—
    When she has walk'd before.

But now her wealth and finery fled,
Her hangers-on cut short all;
The doctors found, when she was dead,—
    Her last disorder mortal.

Let us lament, in sorrow sore,
    For Kent-street well may say,
That had she lived a twelve-month more,—
    She had not died today.

— OLIVER GOLDSMITH

John Wesley Gaines

John Wesley Gaines!
John Wesley Gaines!
Thou monumental mass of brains!
Come in, John Wesley
For it rains.

— ANONYMOUS

Lizzie Borden

Lizzie Borden took an axe
And gave her mother forty whacks;
When she saw what she had done
She gave her father forty-one!

— ANONYMOUS

The Man with the Hoe

Written after seeing Millet's world-famous painting

God made man in His own image
in the image of God made He him.
— Genesis

Bowed by the weight of centuries he leans
Upon his hoe and gazes on the ground,
The emptiness of ages in his face,
And on his back the burden of the world.
Who made him dead to rapture and despair,
A thing that grieves not and that never hopes,
Stolid and stunned, a brother to the ox?
Who loosened and let down this brutal jaw?
Whose was the hand that slanted back this
        brow?
Whose breath blew out the light within this
        brain?

Is this the Thing the Lord God made and
        gave
To have dominion over sea and land;

To trace the stars and search the heavens for
    power;
To feel the passion of Eternity?
Is this the Dream He dreamed who shaped
    the suns
And marked their ways upon the ancient
    deep?
Down all the stretch of Hell to its last gulf
There is no shape more terrible than this—
More tongued with censure of the world's
    blind greed—
More filled with signs and portents for the
    soul—
More fraught with menace to the universe.

What gulfs between him and the seraphim!
Slave of the wheel of labor, what to him
Are Plato and the swing of Pleiades?
What the long reaches of the peaks of song,
The rift of dawn, the reddening of the rose?
Through this dread shape the suffering ages
    look;
Time's tragedy is in that aching stoop;
Through this dread shape humanity betrayed,
Plundered, profaned and disinherited,
Cries protest to the Judges of the World,
A protest that is also prophecy.

O masters, lords and rulers in all lands,
Is this the handiwork you give to God,
This monstrous thing distorted and soul-
  quenched?
How will you ever straighten up this shape;
Touch it again with immortality;
Give back the upward looking and the light;
Rebuild in it the music and the dream;
Make right the immemorial infamies,
Perfidious wrongs, immedicable woes?

O masters, lords and rulers in all lands,
How will the Future reckon with this Man?
How answer his brute question in that hour
When whirlwinds of rebellion shake the
  world?
How will it be with kingdoms and with
  kings—
With those who shaped him to the thing he
  is—
When this dumb Terror shall reply to God,
After the silence of the centuries?

   — EDWIN MARKHAM

Elsie Marley

Elsie Marley is grown so fine,
She won't get up to feed the swine,
But lies in bed till eight or nine,
Lazy Elsie Marley.

— ANONYMOUS

Madame Dill

Madame Dill
Is very ill,
And nothing will improve her,
Until she sees
The Tuileries
And waddles through the Louvre.

— ANONYMOUS

Father William

"You are old, Father William," the young
      man said,
  "And your hair has become very white;
And yet you incessantly stand on your head—
  Do you think, at your age, it is right?"

"In my youth," Father William replied to his
      son,
  "I feared it might injure the brain;
But now that I'm perfectly sure I have none,
  Why, I do it again and again."

"You are old," said the youth, "as I
      mentioned before,
  And have grown most uncommonly fat;
Yet you turned a back somersault in at the
      door—
  Pray, what is the reason of that?"

"In my youth," said the sage, as he shook his
      gray locks,
  "I kept all my limbs very supple
By the use of this ointment—one shilling the
      box—
  Allow me to sell you a couple."

"You are old," said the youth, "and your jaws
    are too weak
    For anything tougher than suet;
Yet you finished the goose, with the bones
    and the beak;
    Pray, how did you manage to do it?"

"In my youth," said his father, "I took to the
    law,
    And argued each case with my wife;
And the muscular strength which it gave to
    my jaw,
    Has lasted the rest of my life."

"You are old," said the youth; "one would
    hardly suppose
    That your eye was as steady as ever;
Yet you balanced an eel on the end of your
    nose—
    What made you so awfully clever?"

"I have answered three questions, and that is
    enough,"
    Said his father; "don't give yourself airs!
Do you think I can listen all day to such stuff?
    Be off, or I'll kick you down-stairs!"

— LEWIS CARROLL

How Pleasant to Know Mr. Lear

How pleasant to know Mr. Lear!
　Who has written such volumes of stuff!
Some think him ill-tempered and queer,
　But a few think him pleasant enough.

His mind is concrete and fastidious,
　His nose is remarkably big;
His visage is more or less hideous,
　His beard it resembles a wig.

He has ears, and two eyes, and ten fingers,
　Leastways if you reckon two thumbs;
Long ago he was one of the singers,
　But now he is one of the dumbs.

He sits in a beautiful parlor,
　With hundreds of books on the wall;
He drinks a great deal of Marsala,
　But never gets tipsy at all.

He has many friends, laymen and clerical,
　Old Foss is the name of his cat;
His body is perfectly spherical,
　He weareth a runcible hat.

When he walks in a waterproof white,
   The children run after him so!
Calling out, "He's come out in his night-
   gown, that crazy old Englishman, oh!"

He weeps by the side of the ocean,
   He weeps on the top of the hill;
He purchases pancakes and lotion,
   And chocolate shrimps from the mill.

He reads, but he cannot speak, Spanish,
   He cannot abide ginger beer:
Ere the days of his pilgrimage vanish,
   How pleasant to know Mr. Lear!

— EDWARD LEAR

FROM

Pocahontas

Wearied arm, and broken sword
Wage in vain the desperate fight;
Round him press a countless horde,
He is but a single knight.

Hark! a cry of triumph shrill
Through the wilderness resounds,
As, with twenty bleeding wounds,
Sinks the warrior, fighting still.

Now they heap the funeral pyre,
And the torch of death they light;
Ah! 'tis hard to die by fire!
Who will shield the captive knight?
Round the stake with fiendish cry
Wheel and dance the savage crowd,
Cold the victim's mien and proud,
And his breast is bared to die.

Who will shield the fearless heart?
Who avert the murderous blade?
From the throng with sudden start
See, there springs an Indian maid.
Quick she stands before the knight:
"Loose the chain, unbind the ring!
I am daughter of the king,
And I claim the Indian right!"

Dauntlessly aside she flings
Lifted axe and thirsty knife,
Fondly to his heart she clings,
And her bosom guards his life!

In the woods of Powhatan
Still 'tis told by Indian fires
How a daughter of their sires
Saved a captive Englishman.

— WILLIAM MAKEPEACE
THACKERAY

Meg Merrilies

Old Meg she was a Gipsy,
    And liv'd upon the Moors:
Her bed it was the brown heath turf,
    And her house was out of doors.

Her apples were swart blackberries,
    Her currants pods o' broom;
Her wine was dew of the wild white rose
    Her book a churchyard tomb.

Her Brothers were the craggy hills,
    Her Sisters larchen trees—
Alone with her great family
    She liv'd as she did please.

No breakfast had she many a morn,
  No dinner many a noon,
And 'stead of supper she would stare
  Full hard against the Moon.

But every morn of woodbine fresh
  She made her garlanding,
And every night the dark glen Yew
  She wove, and she would sing.

And with her fingers old and brown
  She plaited Mats o' Rushes,
And gave them to the Cottagers
  She met among the Bushes.

Old Meg was brave as Margaret Queen
  And tall as Amazon:
An old red blanket cloak she wore;
  A chip hat had she on.
God rest her aged bones somewhere—
  She died full long agone!

— JOHN KEATS

Miniver Cheevy

Miniver Cheevy, child of scorn,
   Grew lean while he assailed the seasons;
He wept that he was ever born.
   And he had reasons.

Miniver loved the days of old
   When swords were bright and steeds were
      prancing;
The vision of a warrior bold
   Would set him dancing.

Miniver sighed for what was not,
   And dreamed, and rested from his labours;
He dreamed of Thebes and Camelot,
   And Priam's neighbours.

Miniver mourned the ripe renown
   That made so many a name so fragrant;
He mourned Romance, now on the town;
   And Art, a vagrant.

Miniver loved the Medici,
   Albeit he had never seen one;
He would have sinned incessantly
   Could he have been one.

Miniver cursed the commonplace
  And eyed a khaki suit with loathing;
He missed the mediaeval grace
  Of iron clothing.

Miniver scorned the gold he sought,
  But sore annoyed was he without it;
Miniver thought, and thought, and thought,
  And thought about it.

Miniver Cheevy, born too late,
  Scratched his head and kept on thinking;
Miniver coughed, and called it fate,
  And kept on drinking.

— EDWIN ARLINGTON ROBINSON

Clementine

In a cavern in a canyon, excavating for a
    mine,
Dwelt a miner, forty-niner, and his daughter
    Clementine.

CHORUS:

Oh, my darling, oh, my darling, oh, my
  darling Clementine
You are lost and gone forever, dreadful
  sorry, Clementine.

Light she was and like a fairy, and her shoes
  were number nine,
Herring boxes without topses, sandals were
  for Clementine.

Drove her ducklings to the water, every
  morning just at nine,
Hit her foot against a splinter, fell into the
  foaming brine.

Ruby lips above the water, blowing bubbles
  soft and fine,
Alas, for me! I was no swimmer, so I lost my
  Clementine.

In a churchyard, near the canyon, where the
  myrtle doth entwine,
There grow roses and other posies fertilized
  by Clementine.

Then the miner, forty-niner, soon began to
  droop and pine,

Thought he ought to join his daughter, now
  he's with his Clementine.

In my dreams she still doth haunt me, robed
  in garments soaked in brine,
Though in life I used to kiss her, now she's
  dead, I draw the line.

— Anonymous

The Modern Major-General

I am the very model of a modern Major-
  General,
I've information vegetable, animal, and
  mineral;
I know the kings of England, and I quote the
  fights historical,
From Marathon to Waterloo, in order
  categorical;
I'm very well acquainted, too, with matters
  mathematical,
I understand equations, both the simple and
  quadratical;

About binomial theorem I'm teeming with a
      lot o' news,
With interesting facts about the square of the
      hypotenuse.
I'm very good at integral and differential
      calculus,
I know the scientific names of beings
      animalculous.
In short, in matters vegetable, animal, and
      mineral,
I am the very model of a modern Major-
      General.

I know our mythic history—King Arthur's and
      Sir Caradoc's,
I answer hard acrostics, I've a pretty taste for
      paradox;
I quote in elegiacs all the crimes of
      Heliogabalus,
In conics I can floor peculiarities parabolous.
I tell undoubted Raphaels from Gerard Dows
      and Zoffanies,
I know the croaking chorus from the "Frogs"
      of Aristophanes;
Then I can hum a fugue, of which I've heard
      the music's din afore,

And whistle all the airs from that confounded
    nonsense "Pinafore."
Then I can write a washing-bill in Babylonic
    cuneiform,
And tell you every detail of Caractacus's
    uniform.
In short, in matters vegetable, animal, and
    mineral,
I am the very model of a modern Major-
    General.

In fact, when I know what is meant by
    "mamelon" and "ravelin,"
When I can tell at sight a Chassepôt rifle from
    a javelin,
When such affairs as *sorties* and surprises I'm
    more wary at,
And when I know precisely what is meant by
    Commissariat,
When I have learnt what progress has been
    made in modern gunnery,
When I know more of tactics than a novice in
    a nunnery,
In short, when I've a smattering of
    elementary strategy,
You'll say a better Major-Gener*al* has never
    sat a gee—

For my military knowledge, though I'm
    plucky and adventury,
Has only been brought down to the
    beginning of the century.
But still in learning vegetable, animal, and
    mineral,
I am the very model of a modern Major-
    General!

— W. S. Gilbert

Richard Cory

Whenever Richard Cory went downtown,
  We people on the pavement looked at him:
He was a gentleman from sole to crown,
  Clean favored, and imperially slim.

And he was always quietly arrayed,
  And he was always human when he talked;
But still he fluttered pulses when he said,
  "Good morning," and he glittered when he
    walked.

And he was rich—yes, richer than a king,
   And admirably schooled in every grace:
In fine, we thought that he was everything
   To make us wish that we were in his place.

So on we worked, and waited for the light,
   And went without the meat, and cursed the
      bread;
And Richard Cory, one calm summer night,
   Went home and put a bullet through his
      head.

— EDWIN ARLINGTON ROBINSON

The Old Woman

Untidy, squat, and soft old body slack
   The woman sat alone beside her door.
The dog, the past; these friends she does not
      lack
   And beauty cannot grieve her any more.

For all her springs are done. These are but
    days
Soft and warm, "that do a body good."
No man can move her now with any praise;
    She cares no more that she be understood.

    — ANONYMOUS

Captain Jinks

I'm Captain Jinks of the Horse Marines,
I feed my horse on corn and beans,
And sport young ladies in their teens,
    Though a captain in the army.
I teach young ladies how to dance,
How to dance, how to dance,
I teach young ladies how to dance,
    For I'm the pet of the army.

CHORUS:

Captain Jinks of the Horse Marines,
I feed my horse on corn and beans,
And often live beyond my means,
    Though a captain in the army.

I joined my corps when twenty-one,
Of course I thought it capital fun;
When the enemy came, of course I ran,
    For I'm not cut out for the army.
When I left home, mama she cried,
Mama she cried, mama she cried,
When I left home, mama she cried:
    "He's not cut out for the army."

The first time I went out to drill,
The bugle sounding made me ill;
Of the battle field I'd had my fill,
    For I'm not cut out for the army.
The officers they all did shout,
They all did shout, they all did shout,
The officers they all did shout:
    "Why, kick him out of the army."

— ANONYMOUS

Good King Wenceslas

Good King Wenceslas looked out,
  On the Feast of Stephen,
When the snow lay round about,
  Deep, and crisp, and even:
Brightly shone the moon that night,
  Though the frost was cruel,
When a poor man came in sight,
  Gathering winter fuel.

"Hither, page, and stand by me,
  If thou know'st it, telling,
Yonder peasant, who is he?
  Where and what his dwelling?"
"Sire, he lives a good league hence,
  Underneath the mountain;
Right against the forest fence,
  By Saint Agnes' fountain."

"Bring me flesh, and bring me wine,
  Bring me pine logs hither;
Thou and I will see him dine,
  When we bear them thither."
Page and monarch forth they went,
  Forth they went together;

Through the rude wind's wild lament,
   And the bitter weather.

"Sire, the night is darker now,
   And the wind blows stronger;
Fails my heart, I know not how,
   I can go no longer."
"Mark my footsteps, good my page;
   Tread thou in them boldly;
Thou shalt find the winter's rage
   Freeze thy blood less coldly."

In his master's steps he trod,
   Where the snow lay dinted;
Heat was in the very sod
   Which the saint had printed.
Therefore, Christian men, be sure,
   Wealth or rank possessing,
Ye who now will bless the poor,
   Shall yourselves find blessing.

— JOHN MASON NEALE

Lincoln

Hurt was the nation with a mighty wound,
And all her ways were filled with clam'rous
  sound.
Wailed loud the South with unremitting grief,
And wept the North that could not find relief.
Then madness joined its harshest tone to
  strife;
A minor note swelled in the song of life
Till, stirring with the love that filled his
  breast,
But still unflinching at the right's behest
Grave Lincoln came, strong-handed, from
  afar—
The mighty Homer of the lyre of war!
'Twas he who bade the raging tempest cease,
Wrenched from his harp the harmony of
  peace,
Muted the strings that made the discord,
  Wrong,
And gave his spirit up in thund'rous song.
O mighty Master of the mighty lyre,
Earth heard and trembled at thy strains of
  fire:

Earth learned of thee what Heav'n already
      knew,
And wrote thee down among her treasured
      few!

— PAUL LAURENCE DUNBAR

Abraham Lincoln

[APRIL 26, 1865]

Oh, slow to smite and swift to spare,
    Gentle and merciful and just!
Who, in the fear of God, didst bear
    The sword of power, a nation's trust!

In sorrow by thy bier we stand,
    Amid the awe that hushes all,
And speak the anguish of a land
    That shook with horror at thy fall.

Thy task is done; the bond are free:
    We bear thee to an honored grave,

Whose proudest monument shall be
   The broken fetters of the slave.

Pure was thy life; its bloody close
   Hath placed thee with the sons of light,
Among the noble host of those
   Who perished in the cause of Right.

— WILLIAM CULLEN BRYANT

Washington

Soldier and statesman, rarest unison;
High-poised example of great duties done
Simply as breathing, a world's honors worn
As life's indifferent gifts to all men born;
Dumb for himself, unless it were to God,
But for his barefoot soldier eloquent,
Tramping the snow to coral where they trod,
Held by his awe in hollow-eyed content;
Modest, yet firm as Nature's self; unblamed
Save by the men his nobler temper shamed;
Not honored then or now because he wooed

The popular voice, but that he still withstood;
Broad-minded, higher-souled, there is but
    one
Who was all this and ours and all men's—
    Washington.

— JAMES RUSSELL LOWELL

Index of Authors

Index of Titles

Index of First Lines

Permissions Acknowledgments

Grateful acknowledgment is made to the following for permission to reprint previously published material:

Estate of Norma Millay Ellis: "What Lips My Lips Have Kissed, and Where, and Why" from *Collected Poems* by Edna St. Vincent Millay (Harper and Row). Copyright 1922 by Edna St. Vincent Millay and Norma Millay Ellis. Copyright renewed 1950 by Edna St. Vincent Millay and Norma Millay Ellis. Reprinted by permission.

Harcourt Brace Jovanovich, Inc.: "Chicago" and "Fog" from *Complete Works of Carl Sandburg* by Carl Sandburg. Copyright 1916 by Holt, Rinehart and Winston, Inc. Copyright renewed 1944 by Carl Sandburg. Reprinted by permission of Harcourt Brace Jovanovich, Inc.

Henry Holt and Company, Inc.: "Stopping by Woods on a Snowy Evening" and "The